# ESTATE AND FINANCIAL PLANNING

## FOR PEOPLE LIVING WITH COPD

MARTIN M. SHENKMAN, CPA, MBA, JD

**demos**HEALTH

**Visit our website at www.demoshealth.com**

ISBN: 978-1-936303-34-2

e-book ISBN: 978-1-617051-35-7

Acquisitions Editor: Noreen Henson

Compositor: diacriTech

Financial information provided by Demos Health, in the absence of a consultation with a financial professional, must be considered as an educational service only. This book is not designed to replace a professional's independent judgment. Our purpose is to provide you with information that will help you make your own financial decisions.

The information and opinions provided here are believed to be accurate and sound, based on the best judgment available to the author and publisher. The publisher is not responsible for errors or omissions. The author and publisher welcome any reader to report to the publisher any discrepancies or inaccuracies noticed.

**Library of Congress Cataloging-in-Publication Data**

Shenkman, Martin M.

  Estate and financial planning for people living with COPD / by Martin M. Shenkman.

       p. cm.

  Includes index.

  ISBN 978-1-936303-34-2

  1. Finance, Personal. 2. Estate planning. I. Title.

HG179.S46144 2013

332.024'016–dc23

                              2012026638

Special discounts on bulk quantities of Demos Health books are available to corporations, professional associations, pharmaceutical companies, health care organizations, and other qualifying groups. For details, please contact:

Special Sales Department

Demos Medical Publishing, LLC

11 West 42nd Street, 15th Floor

New York, NY 10036

Phone: 800-532-8663 or 212-683-0072

Fax: 212-941-7842

E-mail: rsantana@demosmedpub.com

Printed in the United States of America by Hamilton Printing.

12 13 14 15 / 5 4 3 2 1

# ESTATE AND FINANCIAL PLANNING

## FOR PEOPLE LIVING WITH COPD

To Richard and Joan Cowlan
for their insight and generosity in making this book possible.

To Dr. Byron M. Thomashow, MD, and John W. Walsh of the COPD Foundation
for their tremendous help and support in this project.

---

All royalties on this book are being donated to the COPD Foundation to help advance its efforts on behalf of all facing the challenges of COPD. For more information about COPD, contact www.copdfoundation.org or 866-316-COPD (2673).

# CONTENTS

# Foreword

As we say at the COPD Foundation: *COPD is mostly preventable, almost always treatable, and someday curable.* Living with COPD requires life changes, and as a result requires different strategies for estate and financial planning, including addressing end-of-life issues. This is often a topic that many people with COPD tend to avoid, but is nonetheless critical for not only our peace of mind, but also for our families and loved ones.

The COPD Foundation is eternally grateful to Martin Shenkman for his ongoing dedication and commitment to educating those living with COPD, our donors, and estate planners on the importance of planned giving for individuals with COPD. While there are a fair number of reference materials related to living with COPD, this book presents a critically important element, estate (financial) and end-of-life planning, and serves as a valuable resource to our COPD community. We acknowledge his donating all royalties from this book to the COPD Foundation.

We realize the incredible potential that strategic, planned giving can provide to accelerate our mission to cure COPD, as millions of people with COPD will have access to this information. Indeed, this book is a wake-up call that makes us realize that we need to take responsibility now to support research that will eliminate the health challenges, for the next generation, that we experience each day. This book represents a step-by-step guide designed to help us be part of the solution for COPD.

Please accept our heartfelt appreciation to everyone who supports the Foundation through planned giving. It's up to all of us to do our part, as exemplified by Richard and Joan Cowlan's generous support for the publication of this book and our research mission.

If you need more information on COPD, the COPD Foundation has a large variety of materials and support available to you by calling the COPD Information Line at 866-316-COPD (2673) or on our website, www.copdfoundation.org. We also have our COPD Health Management Resource (Big Fat Reference Guide), which is available for free at www.copdbfrg.org.

John W. Walsh
Co-Founder and President
COPD Foundation

# INTRODUCTION

## WHAT IS ESTATE (AND FINANCIAL) PLANNING?

Estate and financial planning are about giving you peace of mind about a host of problems that may confront you during your lifetime and affect your loved ones thereafter. Estate planning means planning to protect you from legal, financial, and other problems. It's about a lot more than signing a will. Financial planning is about addressing the full array of investment, retirement, insurance, and other financial-related topics. It's about a lot more than picking a mutual fund. To really protect yourself and your loved ones, a level of depth, detail, personal issues, and more must be addressed for you to develop an estate and financial plan. Everyone needs to do this. *Regardless of your age, wealth, or health, you need to plan.* Estate planning is not only for the wealthy. To the contrary, it's probably more important for the less than wealthy because you have less security. You have to be more careful about protecting what you have. So don't tune out if you aren't related to Richie Rich. Because you (or perhaps a loved one) is living with COPD, planning is even more important for you. While the focus is almost entirely on estate planning, no estate plan will succeed if it is not built on the foundation of a financial plan (and no financial plan will succeed if it is not built on the foundation of a realistic budget). So use this book to help guide you in planning and implementing an estate plan. This book will not serve as a financial planning guide. But unlike most estate planning books that give little if any attention to financial planning, you'll regularly be reminded of how vital it is to integrate financial planning and estate planning.

The steps will be different to address each person's unique circumstances. But there are some common threads that form the backbone of this book and should be in everyone's plan:

**Documents.** You need to have the same documents that everyone else should have. But some of your documents should be modified to address COPD and any other health challenges you have, and they should be tailored to all of your significant personal circumstances. There is a chapter on each of the key documents and each one will point out considerations that a person living with COPD should address.

**Financial plan.** You need a comprehensive financial plan that addresses your financial needs, the impact of your illness, the likely course your illness will take, and other possible scenarios and contingencies for which to plan. This book addresses financial planning only tangentially, as it affects your estate planning. But contrary to how most estate planners operate, estate plans and financial plans are inextricably linked. You really cannot plan your estate if you don't have a financial plan. Conversely, your financial plan, especially if you are living with COPD and perhaps other health challenges, is unlikely to be successful if you don't have a proper estate plan.

## WHY ADDRESS COPD?

Why a book on planning for people living with chronic obstructive pulmonary disease (COPD)? Because, according to various estimates, 13.1 million Americans have been diagnosed with COPD and more than another 12 million are estimated to be living with COPD and remain undiagnosed. That's 25 million plus. Some estimates place the number of Americans living with a chronic lung disease at closer to 35 million. That is nearly one-tenth of the population! So the numbers of people affected makes it important to address planning for this huge segment of the population.

COPD is one of the most common lung diseases and it has a profound impact on those living with it, their families, loved ones, and caregivers. Estate, financial, and related planning for the substantial number of people touched by COPD should take into account how COPD affects their lives, their health, and their finances. This book will tell you how.

Misconceptions about COPD abound. Even many of those affected by the disease and their loved ones misperceive the realities of COPD. COPD is not a disease of elderly male smokers. COPD remains widely misunderstood. Presently, more woman then men are being diagnosed. In recent years, the number of woman dying from COPD has in fact exceeded the number of men dying from the disease. In addition, more than half of those living with COPD are between the ages of 45 and 64. Alpha-1 antitrypsin deficiency can often result in a diagnosis at a much younger age. It is not rare to see someone diagnosed in their late 20s or early 30s with alpha-1. Many with COPD may lose their employment, careers, or businesses at relatively young ages, long before anticipated retirement. However, this is typically at ages where they have already accumulated some wealth. Thus, planning for COPD cannot be reduced to elder law or Medicaid planning. It is more complex and different. But regardless of the realities, the bias the misconceptions create makes planning harder. Hence, the topic of this book becomes more important for you.

Another misconception is that COPD always results in the destruction of lung tissue. COPD is actually an umbrella term for a number of breathing disorders, not all of which will cause lung destruction. Thus, the common assumption of lung destruction is inaccurate. While certain forms of COPD can create significant lung damage, the use of the term "destruction" can be somewhat inflammatory and excessively dire. Also, the different breathing disorders that comprise COPD are sometimes "co-morbid," that is, one disease occurring with another (e.g., chronic bronchitis and emphysema together). Severe asthma probably should also be identified especially where it affects the COPD spectrum.

The Centers for Disease Control and Prevention (CDC) has determined that COPD is now the third leading cause of death in the United States. COPD is the second or third leading cause of disability in the United States. COPD accounts for 58 million lost work days each year. This makes planning for COPD flare-ups an essential consideration of planning for those living with the disease. Yet surprisingly few attorneys, financial planners, or CPAs have any familiarity with COPD, its disease course, or impact on you. You (and there are tens of millions like "you") need to understand the impact of COPD on planning so that you can inform your advisers and be an active participant in planning to ensure that your goals are met.

## WHAT QUESTIONS DO YOU HAVE?

What questions do you have about estate and financial planning? Like most consumers you are likely barraged with misinformation, too often from someone endeavoring to sell you a service or product. Your personal struggles, with COPD or otherwise, raise practical issues that must be addressed. What steps should you take? How can you get your questions answered? What special steps should you consider in light of COPD? What documents do you need? If the process is handled appropriately, your questions should be answered. If you're not getting your questions answered, make sure you ask them again. If you've asked and are not getting answers, reassess the professionals you hired. To keep costs down and meetings shorter and more organized, try typing up the questions in advance for your advisers to review.

## CHALLENGES YOU MUST FACE TO PLAN

If you are living with COPD, you face many of the same estate and financial planning challenges everyone faces. You will have to address some of the common issues and struggles people living with any chronic illness have to deal with. Finally, you will have to tackle some issues unique to COPD, and in particular your experience with COPD. To be as relevant and complete as possible, this book will tackle many of the issues from each of these categories.

## HOW DOES COPD AFFECT MY PLANNING AND PLANNERS?

Until medical science can restore damaged lung tissue, COPD will continue for your lifetime, and may worsen over time. So your planning must not only integrate steps to address your current status, but it should contemplate the potential for your condition to worsen over time. Thus, to best help you, your advisers must understand your current condition, your anticipated rate of decline, and your future prognosis. Just as your medical team will collaborate to stay a step ahead of the disease, similarly, your estate and financial planning team must help you plan to stay a step ahead of the anticipated future course of the disease. Annual meetings to monitor changes and ensure planning remains optimal are ideal.

## I Have Enough to Deal with Already

COPD means increasing health challenges. Exercise, a healthy lifestyle, and adhering to your medical regimen can have a salutary effect and keep you healthier longer. But that all takes tremendous time and energy. "Who has time for all the financial and legal formalities. What I have is good enough!" Dangerous mistake. Health issues are scary for anyone. In time it might mean less control over matters you could formerly deal with. However, putting your financial and legal house in order, getting in place a comprehensive financial plan and the right estate planning documents to protect you, and simplifying your assets so that they are easier to manage as your COPD or other health challenges evolve, will give you assurance and some certainty in what is otherwise an uncertain life. De-stressing yourself over legal and financial matters may itself reduce stress. Handling the process right will empower you and give you peace of mind. That itself may have a beneficial health impact.

## Emotional and Psychological Impact of COPD

Living with COPD, you may experience severe difficulty breathing. At times this might make you feel closed in, and even vulnerable or helpless. This can lead to fear, perhaps panic, and in some instances even an anxiety attack. Getting other issues off your plate, the potential problems a poor estate or financial plan can create, might lessen overall anxiety, but will certainly create a protective safety net you can rely upon.

For most clients living with COPD there should not be an intense time pressure to plan quickly as there may be with other medical diagnoses (e.g., pancreatic cancer). So unless you are quite elderly, or your COPD or other diseases (co-morbidity) are well advanced, there may be time to acclimate to the planning process and ease into the tough personal decisions estate and financial planning often require. But easing into the process doesn't mean ignoring it or putting it off.

COPD can trigger depression and responses that will impede the planning process and will have to be contended with. See Chapter 3.

# HIRE A PRO

While there is a wealth of information and forms on the web, the quality varies dramatically. Use web resources to educate yourself and guide you and your loved ones to make preliminary decisions (who should be in charge of a power of attorney to handle financial matters if you are hospitalized) and gather data (what information should you organize for a meeting with your estate planner, financial planner, or CPA). If you are willing to use the web and resources like this book to do your "homework" before meeting with professional advisers, you'll save money and get a better result. But know full well that a layperson reading online resources cannot possibly develop the depth and breadth of knowledge a specialist with decades of experience will have. You wouldn't use online resources to determine your medical regimen instead of consulting a pulmonologist. The bottom line is you need to:

❖    Consult an attorney specializing in estate planning in the state in which you reside. State laws, and the programs various states afford to those with health issues, differ substantially. Be wary of relying on any website or on a standardized form. Even the sample forms and discussions in this book, although designed and intended to help you get a plan and documents in place, must always be reviewed by an attorney in your state. The generic web documents, while cheap (perhaps their only positive attribute), are not tailored to address the local nuances that a local expert will understand. They are certainly not going to address the challenges that COPD posses.

❖    Work with a certified public accountant (CPA). If you feel you can prepare your own tax returns using one of the commercially available software packages to save money, great. But just as with an attorney you cannot possibly gain the knowledge or perspectives of an experienced CPA. At minimum you can consult with a CPA to review your income tax return and overall financial picture. It's not only about filing a tax return, it could be about a range of important planning considerations that may be important for you to address. Have you taken maximum advantage of the various income tax deductions that may be available for your treatments? Medications? Home modifications and more? A CPA may identify other tax and investment issues that could be valuable to you. Most CPAs have a broad financial background and will often identify ancillary planning issues that your financial planner might not.

❖    Use a financial planner. There are a number of very large and reputable financial firms that offer products at discounted rates. Some of these have grown tremendously in terms of the depth of investments, services, and other resources they provide. Even if you believe you're capable of managing your own investments and want to avoid commissions or percentage asset management fees, involve a pro. At minimum have a consultation with a financial planner to review your investment allocations. Investment planning is about much more than just picking mutual funds or bonds. You have to make sure you get an independent confirmation that you're on track for what the future may bring.

## WATCH YOUR BACK

Why do you need to spend the money on a pro? One attribute every professional adviser has that you don't is independent perspective. No matter how good you are, you will never see every facet of your own situation. It is just not possible. This is book number 41 for me. I'm a CPA. I hold a PFS credential in financial planning from the American Institute of CPAs. I have an MBA in finance. I hold the designation of Accredited Estate Planner (AEP). But I work with a CPA, and a wealth manager. I try to heed their advice because I know that it is simply too easy to overlook important issues that someone who is "outside" and objective can identify. If I realize a value by hiring professionals, so will you. You can certainly use the approaches mentioned above to keep costs down. You can use all the ideas and recommendations in this book to save money on hiring a pro. But don't, as the proverbial saying goes, "be penny wise and pound foolish."

One more extremely important point. After the economic meltdown of 2008–2009, everyone is wary. You can't turn on a TV or read a news report without seeing yet another supposedly professional investment manager, attorney, or other adviser that was ripping clients off. The way to safeguard yourself is not by avoiding advisers. It's by being proactively involved in your planning. Many consumers believe they can hire a professional and wash their hands of responsibility. Big mistake. You'll get the best results, save the most money, and watch your own back if you stay actively involved in your planning. Any good and honest professional will guide you as to the best ways to do that. One of the other key lessons from the many scams that plagued Wall Street and beyond is "sunlight." Any adviser that is reluctant to let other advisers understand what they are doing is an adviser worth firing. Advisers that are accommodating to letting the sun shine on their efforts, that is, letting your other advisers see what they are doing, are likely to be doing the right job for you. So to really protect yourself, stay involved, and be sure your advisers speak and coordinate. This does not have to add a lot of cost to your professional bills. It might be as simple as a 30-minute phone conference a year where your advisers review the planning for you.

## PLANNING OFFICE VISITS WITH YOUR ADVISERS

You know the challenges you face. Your new attorney won't. Even a long-time CPA you've worked with for decades may not understand COPD (he or she may not even realize you have COPD). Be proactive and discuss with your advisers (or perhaps the secretary or assistant who books your appointment) your condition and what it might mean to a meeting you are scheduling. With a modicum of planning and effort, your advisers can make meetings with you easier, more pleasant, and hence more productive. As with any health issue, your disease and experiences are unique, so being open and forthright as to what accommodations or simple considerations might be helpful is a prerequisite to your advisers' understanding. Consider the following checklist for some ideas of some of the requests you might make:

❖     Might your condition result in common office scents constituting respiratory irritants that could be uncomfortable, or even dangerous? If so, request that the professional and any staff that will be working with you be informed that excessive perfume, cologne, or hairspray could prove a dangerous irritant for you and that they should endeavor to be mindful of how much they use the day of the meeting.

❖     Will strong vapors irritate your lungs and create increased difficulties? If the reception or conference room you will use has infusers, which are common in many offices, perhaps request that they be removed the day prior to your meeting.

❖     Inquire as to whether the office was recently painted, fumigated, or had carpets cleaned with a cleaning solution. If this might pose a serious problem for you, ask to use a different conference room or office, or reschedule your meeting to a later time after the vapors should have dissipated.

❖     Consider writing a short letter explaining that you have COPD, what it means, and how modest accommodations might protect you. For example, no one likes being around someone with a cold or the flu, especially when they are sneezing and dripping. But while that might create a minor nuisance for others, because of your COPD it could trigger a flare-up that could have significant health ramifications. Lung tissue is lost as a result of a flare-up and that tissue cannot be regenerated, so the loss would be permanent. Advance precaution is the compassionate and human response so don't be shy to ask for it. You might request that anyone that has a cold or flu not meet with you.

❖     Many living with COPD are self-conscious about using supplemental oxygen with the exposed cannula (the tube from the oxygen canister to your nose). You might mention or explain any supplemental oxygen equipment you'll bring and any needs it creates. If the particular supplemental oxygen will last for a limited duration that might affect the meeting, or perhaps your need for access to an electrical outlet, let the firm know in advance. Since this might affect meeting time, it's only fair to give the adviser advanced notice.

❖     If it might safeguard you, request that the firm place hand sanitizers in the office and encourage their use by staff before meeting with you. These can be purchased for a nominal amount and be left inconspicuously on conference room tables, and so on. There is no reason that this cannot be done if this will give you peace of mind.

❖     If you will require water, or perhaps a warm beverage (e.g., coffee or hot water for tea) to deal with coughing, mucus, and so on, ask for it. While some firms have hot and cold beverages as standard at any client meeting, many do not.

❖     If you might become too fatigued for a long meeting, let the office know in advance what the maximum duration of your energy might be. That will help the advisers plan the content and flow of the meeting.

## Summary

Estate and financial planning are as vital to your personal financial and legal security as a compliant patient is to the success of your medical regimen. You need to plan. The sooner you tackle planning, the better the results and the easier the process. Keep in mind it is a process, not a one-shot "magic bullet" signing of documents. With tens of millions of people living with COPD, any adviser you hire should be more than willing to accommodate your needs and tailor your planning and documents to address the challenges COPD creates for you. If they are not, move on to other advisers. Think through your concerns and questions in advance to get the most out of any meetings, and to ensure that your needs are addressed. Disclose and discuss what worries you. No one can help you if you don't explain what you personally need for peace of mind, how COPD affects you, and what your goals are. Remember that the most important question in estate and financial planning is "what if?" Ask lots of questions, make sure you understand the answers, and also make sure that in the end, you find the steps to lead you to the "comfort zone" you want and deserve.

## CHAPTER 1

# Nine Steps of Estate (and Financial) Planning

## Introduction to the Nine Steps

IF YOU OR A LOVED ONE UNDERTAKES ESTATE AND FINANCIAL PLANNING, there are nine key steps to consider in the process. These steps are discussed below, and then followed by a more detailed discussion of how these steps change if you (or your loved one) is living with COPD as approximately 25 million Americans are. The difference between how these steps are applied for people in general and those with COPD will help highlight the special nature of planning for those living with COPD.

## Nine Estate (and Financial) Planning Steps to Protect Everyone

### KEY

> There are nine key estate planning steps that everyone needs to take to protect themselves from a wide range of estate and financial planning issues and problems. After this general discussion, these concepts will be evaluated from the perspective of how to address them when you have COPD.

### ○ STEP 1: ORGANIZE FINANCIAL, LEGAL, TAX, AND EMERGENCY INFORMATION

In an emergency, will your family and loved ones know where key legal, tax, and financial information is? Unless you make an effort to organize these records and communicate the information, they won't. Signing a power of attorney to authorize someone to take legal and financial actions for you may not be of much practical help if they cannot figure out where your bank accounts are. You'll never be able to ascertain your current asset allocation (how your investments are allocated among different types of investments) if you don't have an organized picture of your accounts. Organizing and communicating information is important to your plan succeeding. Take the time to make sure the crucial information that may be needed in an emergency is organized, available, and simple.

## ○ STEP 2: CREATE A BUDGET AND DEVELOP A FINANCIAL AND INVESTMENT PLAN

Most people will go to a lawyer (or worse, a legal website) and "get" a will. Bad move. What assurance can a will give if there is no plan as to how money will be spent or invested? You cannot really know what you can gift to help out a child or other loved one if you don't know what you have, what you'll need, and what you'll likely have in the future. So here's the boring drill. Start with a budget. What do you spend now? How does it break out by different categories and types of expenditures? What potentially significant future expenses might you have (grandchild's college? hoped for vacation condo? new car?) that should be factored into your budget? Once you have a budget you can look at your cash inflows (salary, interest, dividends, Social Security, etc.) and determine your current financial situation. You have to evaluate your savings (or spending) rate in light of your assets and future anticipated needs. Based on these and other parameters you can determine an investment plan (how much return you need to achieve your goals and the level of risk you will need to expect to achieve that return over your anticipated time frame). You can then review the results and modify your expenditures, investments, and so on, until the numbers come into line. Without this foundation you cannot properly construct an estate plan, plan for disability, and so forth.

## ○ STEP 3: REVIEW ALL INSURANCE COVERAGE

Insurance is part of the foundation of every plan. It is not only life insurance, but all types of insurance coverage. Consider:

❖     Life insurance coverage can create an estate, pay off mortgages, or other debts, transition a family business, and more. Regardless of whether you're currently insurable, if you have existing insurance it needs to be reviewed.

❖     Disability insurance to substitute for earnings if you cannot work.

❖     Long-term care coverage to cover the costs of nursing homes and in-home care.

❖     Property insurance to cover the replacement cost of assets you own.

❖     Liability coverage to protect you from lawsuits and claims.

❖     Personal excess liability coverage (also called "umbrella" coverage) to provide protection from lawsuits for amounts larger than the limits on your homeowners or automobile coverage.

## ○  STEP 4: DESIGNATE A PERSON TO HANDLE FINANCIAL AND LEGAL ISSUES

If you cannot get to the bank to take care of deposits or bills, how will these important issues be tended to? While practical steps such as online bill paying and automatic deposit of checks can help, they are never enough to rely on. What you need is a legal document, called a power of attorney, in which you can designate a person to handle important legal, tax, and other matters in your place.

## ○  STEP 5: DESIGNATE A PERSON TO MAKE HEALTH CARE DECISIONS AND ACCESS MEDICAL RECORDS

If you undergo surgery, have an accident, or are rushed into hospital with a medical emergency, who can make medical decisions for you? Once you're an adult, generally no one has the right to make health care and related decisions for you unless you give them that right. In order to do that, you need a legal document, called a health care proxy (or "medical power of attorney"). Unless you take the time to prepare an appropriate document, you cannot be assured that your health care wishes will be carried out. In some instances you won't need anyone to take over decision making for you, but you may want a trusted friend or family member to monitor your care. For them to have access to your medical records, you will have to provide them with a special authorization to do so. This authorization must address the requirements of the Health Insurance Portability and Accountability Act (HIPAA) and is called a "HIPAA Release."

## ○ STEP 6: COMMUNICATE YOUR HEALTH CARE WISHES

While it is vitally important that you designate someone to make health care decisions for you in case of an emergency, that alone is not enough. What if a decision has to be made at 2:00 a.m. on a holiday weekend and none of the people you've designated can be reached? How do the physicians caring for you know what your wishes are? Even if your designated decision maker is able to be reached, does that person really know and understand what you would want? And even if he or she does, how difficult emotionally will it be to make the tough decisions? To take care of all these issues, you should prepare a legal document, called a living will, to make your health care wishes known.

## ○ STEP 7: PLAN AND EXECUTE BENEFICIARY DESIGNATIONS AND REVIEW OWNERSHIP OF ASSETS

How you own your assets ("title") is vitally important to all of your planning. If you have an account in a joint name, that might facilitate the person you name using the funds to help you. It also ensures that upon your death, the assets in that account will pass to the person named ("joint tenants with rights of survivorship"). Who you list as the beneficiary of an IRA or life insurance policy will generally determine who will receive that IRA or the proceeds of the life insurance when you die. For many people, how they title assets and who they list as beneficiary will control the distribution of most or even all of their property, not their will. Assets that pass outside of a will are referred to as "non-probate" assets.

## ○ STEP 8: SIGN A WILL

Everyone knows what a will is. It is a legal document to designate where your assets should be distributed in the event of your death. If you have minor children, your will should also name persons to care for your children (guardians).

## ○ STEP 9: CREATE A REVOCABLE LIVING TRUST

A revocable living trust is an arrangement that you make to transfer some or all of your assets to a trust during your lifetime so that on your death those assets won't be subject to the court process (called "probate") of distributing assets in accordance with your will, or in accordance with state law, called "intestacy," if you die without a will.

KEY

> ⚷　While the steps are the same even if you are living with COPD, there are important differences that you need to address because of the difficulties created by your illness. The discussions throughout the rest of this book will provide you with the planning ideas and tools to address your needs. But bear in mind throughout, state laws differ significantly, tax and other laws change frequently, and everyone's personal circumstances are unique. You should always consult with an estate planning specialist in your area.

## RECONSIDERING THE NINE ESTATE (AND FINANCIAL) PLANNING STEPS TO PROTECT SOMEONE WITH COPD

If you are living with COPD, you must still take the same nine key steps to protect yourself and your assets. But there are important differences you need to address due to your medical condition.

### THE FIRST STEP: COME TO TERMS WITH THE EMOTIONAL REALITIES OF YOUR HEALTH STATUS

Your comfort level in dealing with the particular issues that confront your health, future, and end-of-life decisions is vital. Your feelings will vary tremendously, based on your personal disposition, on the nature of your diagnosis, the progress of your illness, and how recently you were diagnosed. If you were recently diagnosed you may be overwhelmed by the myriad of emotions and worries. You may not be forthcoming about the realities of your situation and the need to plan. These hurdles have to be addressed to move forward. When selecting professionals to work with, be sure they are understanding and sensitive to your needs or the process may never get out of the starting block.

EXAMPLE • *Recently Diagnosed with COPD*

Assume Jane Smith, age 50, was recently diagnosed with COPD. Jane works full time in retail where the hours, especially during holiday time, can be

grueling. Jane also has an elderly mother she cares for and other family
responsibilities. Coming to terms with the diagnosis and having to make
pretty radical lifestyle changes to adhere to her physician's recommendations,
Jane is overwhelmed. Jane, as would be expected, is still struggling
emotionally from the news of her diagnosis. In contrast to a disease like
Alzheimer's for which the time period until competency may wane is quite
limited, most people with COPD, subject to other health challenges they
may face, have relatively normal life expectancies. So Jane may not even feel
a time pressure to address planning. That might prove a mistake. There are a
host of financial and estate planning steps Jane should take, some might be
important to take quickly:

❖    Jane should have her life insurance policies reviewed immediately.
She might have term policies that permit conversion to permanent
coverage. With her new diagnosis, new insurance may be costly or not
obtainable. If her existing term coverage (life insurance that lasts only for
a specified number of years) ends soon, converting to a permanent policy
if her existing policy permits, may be the only way to ensure future life
insurance.

❖    Jane should reassess her entire financial plan. Before her diagnosis,
she may have anticipated working full time until a retirement age under
her company's policy of 67. She might now find that retiring early may be
necessary. She may also have to cut her hours back generally, but especially
during peak retail seasons. This might affect her earnings and possibly
employment. The sooner Jane addresses these realities and adjusts her budget
and investment plan, the greater the likelihood she can still reach reasonable
retirement goals.

❖    The risk of a flare-up is such that it behooves Jane to meet with
her attorney and get a durable power of attorney in place so someone
can manage her finances. Similarly, Jane should have the various medical
documents discussed above (health proxy, living will, and HIPAA release)
in place so that if she is hospitalized during a flare-up, her close friend can
make decisions and assist.

## ○  STEP 1: ORGANIZE EMERGENCY INFORMATION

Organizing emergency information is essential for everyone. However,
because some of the symptoms or challenges of COPD, organization is

now even more important than before your diagnosis. It becomes not only a useful tool for those who may help you in a future emergency, but it becomes a tool that you can use to maintain control over your legal, tax, and financial matters, in spite of some of the disease-related difficulties you face. While COPD generally does not result in cognitive impairment, oxygen deprivation can have a debilitating effect. So planning well in advance of that is always advisable. Simplifying your financial affairs and automating as many as possible will minimize the responsibilities and stress, making it easier to cope as your disease progresses or through a flare-up. Thus, organizing information cannot be a static process or occasional event. Many estate and financial planning books give readers practical forms to organize lists of their financial accounts. For those struggling with a COPD, that type of list may not suffice. You need techniques to organize your financial records while you continue to use them, as well as to provide them to family and loved ones in a future emergency. (See Chapter 4.)

## ○ STEP 2: CREATE A BUDGET AND DEVELOP A FINANCIAL AND INVESTMENT PLAN

While a budget and financial plan is critical for anyone seeking to be financially prudent, with your diagnosis of COPD, revisiting and monitoring your budget is even more important to securing your financial future and estate. Consider the example above of Jane Smith who was recently diagnosed with COPD. Consider all the possible ways your planning could be affected by COPD:

❖ Will you have to curtail hours at work?

❖ Will your anticipated retirement age accelerate?

❖ Will you incur additional costs (gym memberships, more costly dietary foods, medical costs not covered by insurance)?

❖ Might you have to modify your home at some future date to make it easier? Perhaps you might even move to a new home in a new area where the weather and air quality are more supportive. What might that cost?

❖ What type of health insurance coverage do you have and what costs might not be covered?

## ◯  STEP 3: REVIEW ALL INSURANCE COVERAGE

If you're facing the challenges of COPD you want to review all of your insurance coverage in light of that reality.

❖    As illustrated in the example of Jane Smith, review your life insurance to see if there are any options under existing policies. Might you still be able to obtain reasonable cost coverage under a group plan?

❖    If you have long-term care coverage, what types of benefits will it provide? If you don't have coverage, is it still feasible to obtain coverage? There is no cost or harm in applying to be sure and do so before your health conditions worsen.

❖    Do you have disability insurance? Are there any reporting requirements under the policy? When might you qualify for benefits? What steps must you meet to do so?

## ◯  STEP 4: DESIGNATE A PERSON TO HANDLE FINANCIAL AND LEGAL ISSUES

If you cannot get to the bank to take care of deposits or bills, how will these important issues be tended to? If your spouse, partner, or other significant person, perhaps even a caregiver, may help you with these tasks, what is your contingency plan if they can no longer help? With COPD you might, as a result of fatigue and other issues, need help for a decade or much longer. While a healthy person your age might name one person and a successor to manage assets during some unanticipated future disability, you might be better served naming three or more alternates to ensure protection over a potentially long disease course.

While everyone needs a power of attorney, you need more specific contingency planning. You must be certain that your power of attorney is "durable," which means that disability won't prevent it from being valid. Many power of attorney forms only become effective if you become disabled. But with COPD, you may suffer a flare-up and need help *now*, but be able to manage your affairs shortly thereafter. The agent you select, depending on your experience of COPD, may be required to take over sporadically over a period of time, or may not be required for several years but will eventually be full time. It is important to have this in mind when selecting an agent. You may also require some other provisions tailored to the experience of COPD. Typical power of attorney forms not only don't address this, and might even include provisions that make it difficult to address your circumstances. Chapter 5 discusses these issues and special modifications you need for your power of attorney. In addition to signing a good power of attorney that is tailored to your situation, you need to take some practical steps to simplify and organize your finances.

There are additional simple steps you can take to help yourself and those you will rely on to address the many scenarios your illness may take. One simple step could include having your agent or a loved one receive duplicate copies of your monthly bank or brokerage statement. This will help them monitor your account at no cost and with little effort. If you make a glaring mistake, or stop paying critical bills because of depression, anxiety, or a flare-up, this simple step might alert them to the situation. You might even opt to have the duplicate statement sent to someone other than the agent you named in your power of attorney, so that you have some checks and balances on anyone potentially abusing your money. These, and similar nuances in the documents and planning, can make a significant difference in protecting you and giving you peace of mind.

## ○ STEP 5: DESIGNATE A PERSON TO MAKE HEALTH CARE DECISIONS AND ACCESS MEDICAL RECORDS

Like anyone else, you need a health care proxy document appointing an agent to make health care decisions for you. However, most people select family members or close friends to make these decisions without giving much thought to it. If the immediate family member or close friend you select to be your health care agent doesn't understand the implications of your disease, how can they really make decisions the way you would want? The need to communicate with your agents is vital. If your agents won't take the time to understand the implications of your illness, you may need to think about designating different people.

## ○ STEP 6: COMMUNICATE YOUR HEALTH CARE WISHES

Everyone should prepare a living will specifying their health care and end-of-life decisions. Too many people, however, simply sign short standard forms that include rather generic language stating that they don't want "heroic measures" if they are terminally ill. These simplistic forms will not suffice for you. There are many decisions that you need to communicate that hopefully have nothing to do with dying. Your care while you are alive, and especially if your condition deteriorates, is important to address. Consider donating tissue or organs for research to help other's suffering from COPD. Decisions as to experimental or unproven medical treatment that may allay symptoms should be addressed, and much more. You really need a living will that is tailored to your particular situation and that addresses all your potential decisions. This is vitally important for those living with COPD because many of the standard clauses in common living will forms contradict the treatments you may be using now.

## ○ STEP 7: PLAN AND EXECUTE BENEFICIARY DESIGNATIONS AND REVIEW OWNERSHIP OF ASSETS

While everyone needs to address the ownership of assets and beneficiary designations, bear in mind that how you own assets will have an impact on how easy it is for people you rely on to help you if you need assistance with financial matters. Importantly, as your condition worsens, or merely as you age, the challenges of COPD may make you more vulnerable to financial abuse. So caution in determining who to list on an account is important.

## ○ STEP 8: SIGN A WILL

You need a will just like anyone needs a will. You might wish to include a charitable bequest (gift) to an organization that helped you, or to a particular research facility. Even if your resources aren't large, a bequest is a great way to thank and acknowledge groups that helped you. Notifying the charity today will help them to collect the gift and enhance their record of donors, thereby encouraging more donations.

If your partner or spouse writes a will, they should consider bequeathing assets to you in a trust to provide for their management and, possibly, a special type of trust that preserves those assets from being reached by nursing homes or others (a "special needs trust"). Most general estate planning books don't touch on this vital issue (but devote lots of time to trusts to save taxes, which may not apply to you). Your will, and that of your partner or spouse, must focus on protecting you in light of the issues that COPD has or may create in the future (see Chapter 9).

### ○ STEP 9: CREATE AND FUND A REVOCABLE LIVING TRUST

Creating a revocable living trust may be the ideal estate planning document and strategy to protect you and your assets. This trust could provide the easiest and best way to allow someone to assist you with financial matters, and manage your assets to whatever degree you might need, depending on the current and future status of your health. Properly used, it can help keep you stay in control of your financial and legal decisions longer. See Chapter 10.

### ⚠ CAUTION

The legal and other issues, especially the sample documents and provisions presented in this book, and those provided free of charge on www.chronicillnessplanning.org and www.laweasy.com, are complex issues and legal documents that require the input, guidance, and assistance of a skilled estate planning attorney who is experienced and licensed in the state in which you live. The reality is that many attorneys have limited experience dealing with issues of chronic illness generally, and certainly COPD in particular, so hopefully your review of the ideas and sample provisions and legal documents in this book will help guide them. The unfortunate practical reality is that although every reader of this book really should use an attorney to complete these important legal documents, a financial planner for wealth management, and a CPA for tax returns and related planning, it will just not be practical from a cost perspective. So throughout this book, suggestions on how to minimize costs and professional fees are provided. Remember, the best plan is not the most expensive or the least expensive; it's the plan that is right for you and that is obtained at a cost that is reasonable compared to the benefits obtained. Suggestions will be made that will help address all wealth levels, from the ultra-high net worth client to those at the lower extremes. COPD knows no economic bounds. Wealth is certainly no insulation. So a broad range of planning will be suggested. That being said, and this is a very important caveat and limitation on the scope of this book, Medicaid (nursing home) planning for those in lower economic strata will not be discussed at all. You must consult with an attorney in your state (state laws vary pretty significantly) who is an "elder law specialist." The title is a bit unfortunate because it has nothing to do with age and everything to do with economic circumstances. Similarly, for those in the wealthy range of the economic spectrum, and certainly the ultra-high net worth client, a range of sophisticated estate tax minimization strategies may well be appropriate. Those are similarly not discussed at all. The focus will remain the broad middle ground of integrating the impact of COPD into your general planning. You can then address Medicaid, estate tax planning, and other nuances with your advisers.

KEY

> Every aspect of your planning—financial, estate, documents, insurance, and so on—must be tailored to address the implications of COPD and any other health challenges you have.

## CHAPTER SUMMARY

This chapter has provided an overview of the entire estate planning process by explaining the nine key steps you must take to protect yourself. Importantly, since every aspect of planning changes when you are living with COPD, each of the nine steps has been explained in a manner that applies to you.

## CHAPTER 2

# COPD Estate (and Financial) Planning Basics

## Estate Planning and COPD

IF YOU OR A LOVED ONE HAS COPD, estate and financial planning takes on greater importance and requires modifications from what is typically done for those who don't have a chronic illness. Too often estate planning is viewed as merely signing "standard," or what lawyers affectionately call "boilerplate," forms. While this is dangerous for even the average person, it can be more so for those with COPD and their loved ones. Some "standard" forms just won't work for you. To help you in this process, this book will guide you through the steps you and your loved ones should evaluate. While the nuances of every aspect of your situation cannot possibly be addressed, enough modifications and options to general planning are presented so that you, with the assistance of your advisers, can adapt the steps appropriate for you. Just like those racy car commercials that caution you not to try it at home, you'll need professional help as well. This book will guide you on how to deal with an attorney and estate planner, and, to a lesser degree, other advisers.

### KEY

You need to be proactive. Don't assume that your advisers (attorney, accountant, financial planner, etc.) understand the nuances of COPD or any other illness or health challenge you have. They also may not understand how planning and documents need to be modified for these. You have to inform them. If you're uncomfortable discussing your illness and its potential consequences, bear in mind that if you don't make sure the people advising you really understand, you won't have the protections you or your loved ones need. However difficult, you'll benefit by being forthright, clear, and very specific.

# CHRONIC ILLNESS AFFECTS ESTATE PLANNING

Even though you have a chronic illness, the same estate planning documents and planning techniques used for someone without a chronic illness and of comparable financial and other circumstances will be used. That being said, however, most documents and many aspects of planning should be tailored to address the potential impact of your chronic illness. The nature and magnitude of the changes that are necessary will depend on your personal circumstances, your general medical prognosis, how COPD specifically affects you, the possible range of courses your disease might take, your assets, family, and other personal circumstances. If you are living with COPD, the manner in which your planning should be modified will differ from the modifications of someone living with Parkinson's disease, multiple sclerosis, or Alzheimer's disease. Too often advisers and even loved ones lump all health issues together and assume the same simplistic misconceptions about planning. To best tailor a plan and documents to meet your needs, the nature of the specific disease course anticipated for you needs to be addressed. Helping you do just that is a key goal of this book.

KEY

> Your experience with COPD is unique to you. Thus, while estate planning should consider the potential impact of your particular illness, it should be tailored to address your personal experience and the likely trajectory that your illness will take.

EXAMPLE • *Impact of COPD Diagnosis*

To illustrate planning modifications, let's use a personal experience of someone diagnosed with COPD that was posted on the Internet as a case study.

*Following a battery of tests, including a spirometry and arterial blood gas, my family doctor said, "It's bad, very, very bad." The words didn't scare me as much as the somber look on his face and the sad tone in his voice. "You have severe emphysema," he said, "which is progressive and incurable." The next few minutes were a blur as he explained the diagnosis, interspersed with instructions for the nurse to order oxygen to be delivered to my home that very afternoon.*

*Oxygen! I thought. No, he can't be serious. Too stunned to ask questions, I nodded as he referred me to a pulmonary specialist and told me I needed to be in a pulmonary rehabilitation program.*

*That day my life changed forever. In a blink of an eye, I went from an independent, energetic newspaper editor with a bright future to a disabled, chronically ill patient, who had to rely on oxygen at night and medications by day to breath more easily.*

*I tried to keep up with my fast-paced lifestyle, which now included 3 days a week at pulmonary rehab, but I couldn't. I simply did not have the energy. I took a leave of absence from work and fell into a deep depression.*

A diagnosis of COPD affects every aspect of your estate and financial planning. Some of the modifications are minor, some significant. But in all events, some special planning steps should be implemented immediately. Other planning modifications can be viewed as more long-term goals. One of the problems with addressing planning is that depression, anxiety, guilt, and so many of the emotions that may accompany the diagnosis work against you. If you're a loved one or caregiver for someone living with COPD, perhaps you can take charge and serve as the catalyst for the process. Financial planning to address the implications to job and career need to be addressed. Simplifying, consolidating, and automating financial and other matters to free up time for rehabilitation, support groups, and other steps that will make new demands on your schedule are essential. Putting in place safeguards to minimize financial or other abuse is strongly advisable.

Show the following section to your advisers to help you inform them about COPD and your planning needs.

# EXPLAINING COPD

You'll have to explain how COPD affects you to your professional advisers, and perhaps family and friends who will play a role in your estate and financial planning. It might be helpful to start the conversation by explaining the implications of COPD generally. Then discuss your personal experience with COPD. If this conversation is difficult for you, you might consider showing your adviser or other key people the following overview, then engage them in the discussion about your situation.

COPD may appear in various forms:

- ❖ Chronic bronchitis
- ❖ Refractory asthma
- ❖ Emphysema
- ❖ Bronchiectasis

Some of the above forms may occur in the same person.

Smoking is the primary cause of COPD. Even second-hand smoke can be a factor. But it is not the only factor or cause, and most smokers will never contract COPD. Workers exposed to fumes and other pollutants in the work environment are also at risk for COPD. While there is merit to downplaying the risk factor of tobacco exposure because of other causes of COPD, the reality is that 90% of COPD in America is caused by tobacco exposure. It is also important to note that the onset of COPD symptoms may occur many years after smoking cessation. Just because you stop smoking at 25 doesn't guarantee that you won't develop COPD years later because the damage and progression have already been initiated. However, given the tremendous benefits of ceasing to smoke, that should still remain the focus.

Alpha-1 antitrypsin deficiency (alpha-1) is a genetic condition that is passed from parents to their children. Alpha-1 occurs when there is a lack of a protein in the blood that protects lung tissue. This protein is called alpha-1 antitrypsin, or "AAT," which is primarily produced in the liver. Alpha-1 is currently the most significant known risk factor for COPD but current research suggests that additional genetic predispositions for contracting COPD are being identified.

COPD can often result in damage to the lungs, although not every one of the diseases that come under the umbrella of COPD will. The disease may damage the alveoli, the tiny sac-like ends of the bronchial tubes where oxygen and carbon dioxide are exchanged from the lungs to the bloodstream. COPD can damage the cilia, the hair-like membrane that lines the bronchial tubes leading to the lungs. Since cilia keep debris from reaching the lungs, those with COPD are more likely to experience infection and may have to rely on mechanical means to filter the air they breathe (e.g., room air purifier).

Someone living with COPD will experience shortness of breath and difficulty breathing. This can lead to less oxygen reaching the lungs, bloodstream, and body (called "hypoxia"), and, in some cases, an accumulation of carbon dioxide in the blood (called "hypercarbia"). COPD can trigger asthma-like attacks. Symptoms of COPD can include a cough with mucus, shortness of breath (called "dyspnea"), wheezing manifestations, and other conditions. This should not be confused with the cough one gets with a cold that later resolves. This is a chronic ongoing cough that is symptomatic of a much more significant underlying deterioration. The difficulties the person with COPD has breathing will typically worsen with mild activity. Other physical symptoms may include: fatigue, frequent respiratory infections, wheezing, and so forth. COPD is a chronic illness; it is progressive. It gets worse. There is presently no known cure, although there are a host of treatments that can have a tremendous positive impact.

## Caution to Professional Advisers

Misconceptions about COPD, and chronic illness generally, are common, and very difficult for those living with chronic illness and their loved ones. Don't assume that you as an adviser understand any client's unique circumstances. Make a point of asking the client, and even a caregiver or other family member accompanying the client to a meeting, to explain and educate you. Some major misconceptions include:

❖  *Chronic illness is uncommon.* The reality is that many millions of people are affected. It is not rare or unusual. COPD affects nearly five times as many people as Alzheimer's disease. Yet many people have never heard of it.

❖  *COPD was self-inflicted.* False. COPD is not only caused by smoking. Genetic issues can trigger COPD. Breathing industrial fumes and other toxins can also cause COPD. Even among smokers, the vast majority will not develop COPD. This misconception is often held by your client living with COPD and that can trigger guilt and other negative emotions that can derail the planning process. Be sensitive to these implications.

❖  *Planning is the same.* False. Henry Ford joked that you could have the Model T in any color—as long as it was black. Don't assume planning is the same. There are tremendous variations and nuances. Don't fall into this erroneous assumption. Request that your client inform you of his or her current situation and the likely future consequences. Importantly, many people living with COPD simultaneously struggle with other diseases and health challenges. The combination of these can have a significant influence on longevity, quality of life, and other factors. Be certain to understand the big picture so you can help plan appropriately. Bear in mind that many clients may not understand many nuances of their own conditions.

❖    *Invest short term and use special needs trusts.* These do not hold true for everyone with a chronic disease or disability. Investigate all options. For many people living with COPD, they will have worked much of or even a full career before stopping work. So they may in fact have substantial resources and need planning to address that.

## CHRONICALLY ILL FAMILY MEMBER INCAPABLE OF SIGNING DOCUMENTS

If your loved one is living with COPD, and perhaps another chronic illness, and he or she puts off planning for too long, your loved one may no longer have the ability to sign documents or take informed planning steps. In such situations, you'll be reading this book instead of them. Your loved one's inability doesn't mean the inability to help. It just limits the options and demands different approaches. If, for example, your parent is elderly and has struggled with COPD for years, and has had a number of serious flare-ups, the oxygen deprivation of which has had an impact on his competency too significantly for him to sign a will or other documents, planning must take on a different perspective. Some of these steps are summarized below:

❖    Carefully confirm the mental status of your loved one. In most cases with COPD it should still be feasible to sign a will and likely even other legal documents. But don't assume that COPD does not affect competency. If your loved one can no longer sign legal documents, don't give up on planning; pursue the options that remain.

❖    Determine in consultation with your loved one's caregiver and medical providers if he or she has periods when competency may be improved. It may be possible for a loved one with COPD that has had cognitive issues from long periods of oxygen deprivation to have periods when he or she is more lucid. If so, endeavor to schedule meetings for those times if feasible. If you have to use this approach, be certain to hire an experienced estate attorney to make certain that all the appropriate legal formalities of signing a document during a period of lucidity are addressed.

❖    In order to assist your loved one, you will need access to medical records. Scour existing legal documents and inquire of his or her attending physician and neurologist whether documents authorizing the release of private health information were signed. These are necessary in most circumstances to access a loved one's medical records as a result of HIPAA laws, which are discussed in Chapter 7. If this wasn't done, obtaining the requisite medical information may require your being appointed as a court-appointed guardian (a person designated by the court to handle personal or financial decisions for someone who is incapacitated).

❖    Inventory all assets and liabilities. Pay particular attention to the exact manner in which ownership is worded ("title") and whether beneficiary designation forms (indicating who inherits the asset on death) exist and who is listed. This detail will be critical to determining what might be advisable to do, and what can be done.

❖    Coordinate financial needs with your loved one's financial and estate planners, including addressing the title to financial assets, beneficiary designations, insurance policies, and so on. It may be possible, using the title to certain assets, beneficiary designations, and the ability of well family members and others listed as co-owners or beneficiaries, to decline benefit from those assets (in legal jargon: "disclaim" or "renounce") in order to direct those assets as desired even in the absence of your loved one's ability to sign a new will.

❖    Obtain, read, and analyze all existing estate planning documents with an estate attorney. Determine what options may be utilized in the current situation to better help your loved one. If there is no valid will, evaluate the impact of the state's intestacy laws on the situation. These rules say who should inherit assets when there is no will. If your loved one had signed a durable power of attorney (see Chapter 5) you may want the person named in that document (the "agent") to modify beneficiary designations and title to assets to effect the desired results.

❖    Evaluate the merits of seeking a court-appointed guardianship. For example, your loved one may have a substantial taxable estate and the only flexibility under existing estate planning documents executed prior to his or her becoming incompetent are limited to making annual gifts up to the annual gift exclusion amount ($13,000 that can be given away to any number of people without a gift tax consequence under

2012 law). That limit will hardly make a dent in the taxable estate. Consider whether the powers permit establishing and contributing to a family limited partnership or other entity that may discount values (and the risks of that type of planning). Evaluate the potential for a court conferring on a guardian the right to make more extensive estate planning steps.

❖      For the rest of this book it will generally be assumed that "you" are the reader and the person living with COPD, although some additional planning ideas for your loved ones will be noted, primarily in Chapter 12.

KEY

> ━○━     It is your responsibility to do as Dr. Phil always recommends: "Get real" and lay the cards on the table so your planners can help you instead of relying on their preconceived notions of what your situation might be. If you are reading this book for a family member living with chronic illness, the reality is that many people struggle to come to terms with what their current condition is and how it may affect them in the future. If you really care about this person, you have to guide, encourage, and help. This is especially important if your loved one suffers from illness-related depression or apathy.

# How COPD Affects Estate Planning

There are a host of ways your COPD makes the estate planning process different.

## COMMUNICATE WITH YOUR ATTORNEY AND OTHER ADVISERS

Here are some discussion points to prepare for your estate planner:

❖      What illnesses do you have? Is COPD the only health challenge? What does your diagnosis mean to your current situation and likely future situations?

❖ Is your course of the disease mild, moderate, or severe? What is your current state of disability and how rapidly is it expected to progress? These factors will help indicate time frames for planning, whether a trust should be used, and so on. There are significant differences between various chronic illnesses and even among those living with COPD.

❖ When were you diagnosed?

❖ Are you having any cognitive impairment currently, and, if so, to what extent? You must therefore explicitly explore these issues with your attorney.

❖ Arrange to bring a clarifying letter from your attending physician and neurologist to address the above issues for your attorney.

KEY

> You need to communicate details about your condition to your estate planner and other advisers.

## CHOOSING PEOPLE (FIDUCIARIES) YOU CAN RELY ON

When most people choose an executor (the person to manage their affairs when they die) or a health care agent (the person to make medical decisions if they can't), it's often a theoretical exercise. They generally don't believe death or serious medical decisions are imminent (tempting fate is a favorite pastime for most people who are "fine"). For you, the decisions are real, important, difficult, and, depending on the challenges you are contending with, some decisions could have an imminent impact (e.g., naming a health care agent to address medical decisions if you suffer a flare-up or have surgery scheduled in the near term). This makes these appointments all important to your planning. Almost every legal document discussed in this book is dependent upon a person you designate carrying out your wishes as set forth in the document. The best health care proxy isn't worth much if the person you select to make medical decisions cannot do it, or lacks the knowledge or sensitivity (or both!) that you anticipated.

Most people select immediate family members as agents. However, everyone living with a chronic illness has a very different experience of how their loved ones react to their illness. For example, you may have an estranged sibling who has never come through. Sadly many people abandon a spouse diagnosed with a chronic illness (so much for the vow of "for better or worse…in sickness or health"). Fortunately for some, family and friends become foundations of unwavering support after the diagnosis. Others are unable to deal with the circumstances and are unsupportive; some may virtually disappear from your life because of their discomfort facing your diagnosis or other trivial reasons or perceived slights. These reactions, whichever direction they take, will give you invaluable insight into which people to name as fiduciaries and which to avoid.

No professional adviser can have the insight into how different family, friends, or others you might rely upon will react to your diagnosis. You have to provide the insight or commentary. A professional adviser can provide insight into the characteristics of what might make a good fiduciary. They can provide suggestions for building safeguards in the event you have some concerns over the integrity or capabilities of agents. But you have to provide the details for the analysis. This is why it can be helpful to involve other advisers in the process who have known you and the other family members you are considering for a long time.

COPD, like many chronic illnesses, can be enigmatic. So much remains unknown about the causes, symptoms, and manner in which it may affect you. Family and friends may not believe, or if they believe they may not comprehend or accept, the significant challenges you might face. In these cases, it may be more difficult for you to determine the appropriateness of naming these people as your fiduciaries. A frank and detailed discussion is probably advisable.

The bottom line is that you should not assume that the usual cast of characters should automatically be named to serve as your fiduciaries. Don't let your attorney lead the conversation by suggesting the usual relationships to serve in these capacities if they are not really appropriate for you. Your attorney will have no way of knowing the reactions of your family and loved ones without your input. Discuss your concerns and options. If you are newly diagnosed, you should honestly reevaluate who you designated as fiduciaries in your existing documents in light of how these presumably important people have reacted since your diagnosis.

Because there is no cure, and because your condition may worsen, you have a much greater probability of having to rely on your fiduciaries in vital ways and over a longer time period. It is particularly important for you to select fiduciaries based on what the prospective fiduciaries have demonstrated they can do to assist you, not out of familial obligation. This is no time for decisions motivated by guilt or friendship.

Careful consideration should be given to naming an institutional cotrustee to ensure the fiduciary's long-term viability. This lessens the long-term and potentially significant administrative burdens on a friend or family member who might otherwise have served alone as fiduciary. Don't dismiss naming a bank or trust company because of rumors you've heard about their poor performance or lack of sensitivity. These complaints are incorrect. The real "problem" with institutional trustees that most people have is exactly the reason you should favor an institution. Institutional trustees operate "by the book." What the legal documents provide for is exactly what they are going to do. In contrast, when trusty Uncle Joe is serving as a trustee, he might just do whatever is asked of him. If you are living with COPD, especially if it may eventually affect your cognitive abilities to a degree that you will become dependent on your fiduciaries, you want the integrity and formality of an institutional trustee that will adhere to your wishes. There is no better way to protect yourself. Boilerplate, cheap Internet documents make great commercials, but not much more. Tailored documents, especially a funded revocable living trust, with an institutional trustee, are your best assurance. One step better is to name a trusted family member, friend, or loved one, to serve together with the institution (when multiple trustees serve they are called "co-trustees"). Bear in mind that institutions will serve as executors (to administer your estate), and as trustees (to administer trusts you set up). They cannot serve as agents under your power of attorney (Chapter 5) or health care proxy (Chapter 7).

KEY

> The best way to avoid perceived complaints that people have about institutions is to take the time to carefully tailor your estate planning documents to your needs and wishes.

Selecting fiduciaries if you have a chronic illness has some other nuances to consider:

❖ COPD can be characterized by unpredictable attacks, or flare-ups, lasting for days or weeks. The on–off use of an agent requires fast reaction for short durations with no notice. The agent selected under a power of attorney or health proxy must be appropriate to this unique circumstance. Preparing the agent in advance is also important.

❖ If you have steadily deteriorating COPD, your agent under your durable power of attorney or a successor trustee under a living trust, might have advance notice of the pending need to serve as your condition worsens and in advance of their having to take control of your affairs. This might make an agent who lives further away more feasible than for other chronic illnesses.

❖ Often agents are selected based on their understanding of your major objectives and wishes. However, since you are living with a chronic illness, the focus is different. Your agent under your durable power of attorney, or a successor trustee under a living trust, should be able and willing to handle routine financial and legal details over a long period, not just a few big decisions. Depending on the progression of and your history with COPD, you may have the mental presence to make major decisions, even if those decisions have to wait for a post-surgical recovery or for a flare-up to subside. This is substantially different than the focus for other chronic neurological disorders where significant cognitive impairment is likely (such as Alzheimer's). These factors differentiate planning for COPD from planning for a number of other significant chronic illnesses and may affect who you select as an agent. For example, if you are unlikely to have significant cognitive impairment, you might be more comfortable naming a friend as the co-trustee of your living trust to serve with you since you can monitor their activities.

❖ If you don't face significant cognitive impairment, you might wish to retain the power to replace trustees even if you give up the role of trustee for yourself because of the strain it causes you. For more sophisticated planning, you might use a third party, such as a "trust protector," to provide a check and balance on the trustees.

## COPD May Affect the Timing of Planning

Chronic illness affects the time horizon you have to make decisions and implement planning. It's important to clearly inform your attorney and other advisers of the time line of your illness and, most importantly, of how that illness affects you from a physical, emotional, financial (e.g., costs, impact on earnings ability), and other perspectives. Timing can be critical to estate and financial planning, and too many advisers, unless they've been personally touched by COPD, may not understand the implications. Worse yet, they might tend to make the same erroneous assumptions most people do, and lump all chronic illnesses together as if they all have the same symptoms and implications.

EXAMPLE • *COPD Disease Course*

While the progression of any disease will depend on a host of variables (your health before diagnoses, quality of care, how compliant you are as a patient with your pulmonologist's and other physician recommendations, etc.), some of the general progressions or time frames for COPD will help identify planning time parameters.

❖    A typical disease course for a COPD patient might begin, perhaps a decade after starting to smoke, with mild symptoms that may barely be noticeable.

❖    A chronic cough, might begin with modest sputum.

❖    Shortness of breath during exertion may start to appear.

❖    The shortness of breath becomes more pronounced.

❖    Some degree of airways obstruction develops, but it might in part be reversed.

❖    COPD progresses and most symptoms gradual worsen. The deterioration becomes more evident.

❖    Repeated coughing attacks require longer and longer to recover from.

❖    If severe lung damage develops, difficulty breathing becomes more acute.

❖    Progression and survival are closely related to the level of lung function when diagnosed.

Where you are on the planning spectrum will vary with the point at which you were diagnosed, your age, work status, and so forth. There are nearly as many people believed to be living with COPD who have not yet been diagnosed with the disease, as there are people who have been diagnosed. This means many people living with COPD may not be diagnosed until their disease has progressed quite significantly. For them, the need for planning will have a greater urgency then for those diagnosed earlier in the process. Since attacks, some of which might result in hospitalization, cannot be predicted, some aspects of planning should be treated with urgency by anyone diagnosed with COPD.

# CHRONIC ILLNESS AFFECTS THE ECONOMICS OF PLANNING

How does the disease course of COPD affect the economics of your estate planning? Most advisers erroneously assume that everyone with a chronic illness has limited resources, needs to focus investment planning on liquidity and minimum risk, and should have a non-springing power of attorney, and so on. Some chronic illnesses strike early, truncating even the most lucrative of careers. Others, such as Parkinson's and Alzheimer's, tend to strike at later ages (the young onset versions being an exception). Even some diseases that are diagnosed at an earlier age, such as multiple sclerosis, allow somewhat normal lives, until becoming more severe at a later age. This is important, because an initial diagnosis much later in life may have afforded you the opportunity to earn and save assets through a normal retirement age. Generalizations are dangerous. You must make sure to inform your advisers of your specific circumstances and be sure they plan accordingly. See the discussion in Chapter 12 concerning investment planning for those living with COPD.

## A NOTE TO FAMILY AND CARETAKERS

If your loved one has COPD, your role and importance in his or her estate planning will differ, often markedly, from that of a spouse, partner, or loved one for someone who does not face the same challenges. Your role in serving as a catalyst to get the estate and financial planning process moving may be the most important role you serve.

EXAMPLE • *Emotional Component to COPD*

Somewhat unique to COPD are feelings of remorse, a sense of regret for past actions, particularly smoking. Many people living with COPD blame themselves for their disease. These difficult feelings can be exacerbated by insensitive remarks made by others.

Depression, anxiety, apathy, and other emotional consequences of COPD can have a profound impact. It is vital for you, if your loved one has COPD, to encourage, even push, them to complete planning before the disease progresses to the point of making it more difficult, or perhaps impossible, to implement optimal planning. Fatigue, anxiety, potentially even cognitive impact all may worsen as the COPD progresses. Yet the apathy and depression COPD may create may make your loved one act in the opposite manner of what all logic and caution would indicate. If your loved one is not pursuing the appropriate planning with sufficient earnest, encourage them to move forward. Enlist their neurologist, attorney, and others to support your efforts to get them to address planning. Consider hiring a care manager to review the situation and make recommendations after a home visit.

## Prepare for Your First Meeting with Your Estate Planner

When you prepare for your first meeting with your estate planner, there are some basics steps you can take to make the meeting go more smoothly, productively, and quickly. This will translate into a better result, greater likelihood of achieving your goals, and lower costs (to the extent that your attorney and other planners bill hourly).

❖    *Disease description.* Prepare a summary of how COPD affects you and the anticipated disease course.

❖    *Balance sheet.* Prepare a balance sheet listing your assets (things you own) by category and how they are owned. If feasible, attach copies of the relevant documents to back up the numbers on the balance sheet (e.g., a brokerage statement, deed, etc.). For many of the goals of estate planning it is the "big picture" that must be understood. The balance sheet is really a snapshot, a mile-high picture, at a point in time of what you own and what you owe (liabilities).

❖    *Family data (tree).* An attorney will need a summary of all family members, regardless of your feelings toward them. At a minimum, this should include parents, siblings, children, grandchildren. If anyone is deceased, divorced, has a health issue, is not a United States citizen, indicate this. Also, provide each person's full legal name, nickname if commonly used, Social Security number, address, and age. "Family" is defined differently for everyone. If there are people whom you consider your family, even if they don't follow the pattern of the Cleaver family, list them and explain their relationship. Most estate planning books continue to be written as if June and Ward Cleaver are the prototype American family! The key to avoid the estate problems many people have is to make sure that you take the time to carefully communicate your background information and wishes. Indicate which if any of these people might be appropriate to name as fiduciaries (see below).

❖     *List of trustees, agents, and other fiduciaries.* If you can provide a list of a minimum of one fiduciary and at least two alternates (successors) for each of the estate planning documents discussed in this book, you'll save considerable time. Provide the person's full legal name, nickname if commonly used, address, and age. You might want to note why you have named this particular person, and whether you have any concerns about naming them. This will put your questions squarely on the table for your attorney to address with you quickly and efficiently.

❖     List of intended donees and beneficiaries. Who should inherit? Who should receive gifts? If you are leaving assets unequally (e.g., favoring a child who has been your caretaker), indicate why the difference.

You need to prepare additional information and materials for your planner about COPD. Having these ready and present at your first meeting will also save time and money, and better ensure that your goals are met.

❖     What is your experience of COPD? Be specific.

❖     What are the current symptoms of your illness?

❖     What is your age?

❖     How does age affect your condition?

❖     What insurance coverage do you have?

❖     What other health issues do you have? You need to make sure your estate planner understands the potential course of your illness and your general health since other health issues can accompany your COPD, exacerbate its impact, and accelerate the progression of problems. For example, many people living with COPD also may have diabetes, cardiovascular issues, high blood pressure, and other ailments that may independently cause dementia or other significant detriments.

❖     Are you presently having any cognitive impairment, and if so, to what extent?

❖     Has a care manager, pulmonologist, or other person prepared a report as to your status? Copies of this information might be very useful and will save the time and money of your attorney seeking this information.

❖     COPD can be complicated and variable. You may lack sufficient technical understanding of your own condition and prognosis, or emotions may make it too difficult for you to relate these points. Consider requesting a clarifying letter from your attending pulmonologist to address these matters. Since each person's chronic disease progresses in its own unique manner, some detailed understanding is important to assess the urgency of planning.

❖     Will you need caretaker assistance? When? What plans have been made to address this?

❖     If you have a care plan prepared by a social worker, geriatric consultant, or other specialist, bring a copy as this could be a very informative road map for your estate planner.

## Inform Your Estate Planner How COPD Affects Your Interactions with Them

You should inform your attorney and other advisers of what steps they need to take to modify their practices to accommodate your needs. Letting them know in advance will make the process more comfortable for all. Are there certain times of day—perhaps correlated to the impact of fatigue—that would be preferable to schedule appointments and conference calls? If the weather can have a strong negative impact on how you feel, you might let the advisers know in advance that you might need to reschedule. If you prefer several shorter meetings, or perhaps one longer meeting to limit trips, tell your advisers. If shortness of breath and other symptoms have made you somewhat housebound, tell your advisers. They might rightfully grow concerned over the potential for a caregiver, neighbor, or other person to take advantage of you and thus be alerted to take precautions to protect you from abuse. Unlike the famous Clairol commercial, it should not be that "only your hairdresser knows for sure."

EXAMPLE • *Larger Adviser Role*

What role should your attorney and other advisers play? In most instances, advisors work directly with their client. However, depending on your symptoms and especially as your illness progresses, there may be times when your advisers could help you most by communicating with your fiduciaries (agent under a power of attorney) and loved ones directly. To facilitate this, specific steps to authorize communication with others must be taken. If your illness will eventually result in dementia or substantial incapacity, this point should be addressed when you are first deciding which advisers to retain. You should focus on experienced practitioners who won't abuse the authority to communicate, and who are conscientious enough not to neglect the responsibility you are delegating. As no surprise, the Internet and computer-prepared legal forms not only won't address this nuance, they won't provide this degree of help. Similarly, your family attorney who is nearly 80 years old is not an ideal candidate.

For attorneys, reaching out to family members if not authorized to do so by you, their client, may constitute a violation of attorney ethics so advanced preparation is required. Consider including an "authorization to communicate" in the retainer agreement and even in specific estate planning documents (e.g., a durable power of attorney). See the sample provision in the Introduction to this book.

Similar steps may be advisable to take with your other advisers. For example, you may sign a HIPAA release that permits your insurance consultant to speak with your financial agent or others. The investment policy statement (IPS) you sign with your wealth manager (the document that establishes the manner in which your funds will be invested) might be modified to expressly authorize your wealth manager's communication with your financial agent.

## IF YOU CAN'T AFFORD AN ESTATE PLANNER

Whether your resources are very limited or your estate substantial, this book will give you guidance on how to make sure your planning and documents are crafted to address the special circumstances of COPD and any other health challenges, and help you minimize legal and other professional fees, by guiding you to work most economically with your advisers. However, if you don't have sufficient funds to spend, how can you obtain the benefits of the ideas and sample provisions contained in this book? If you're doing it alone and using a computer program for documents, you can modify those documents to reflect the information, ideas, and sample provisions and forms in this book and those provided on www.chronicillnessplanning.org and www.laweasy.com. However, there is never a substitute for the judgment of an experienced estate planning attorney.

# WHAT THIS BOOK DOESN'T COVER

This book does not address a number of issues that receive much media attention, and that are included in most estate planning books. This is done intentionally, so read on.

## PROBATE

This book doesn't really address probate avoidance to a great extent. Probate is the process by which an estate is settled after someone dies. Too often, avoiding probate becomes the focus of an entire estate plan. While there can be benefits of avoiding probate, sometimes substantial ones, that goal should never be the focus of your estate plan. The primary goal of your estate plan (or if you are a Star Trek fan, the "Prime Directive") is to take care of *you*. Probate only occurs when you die. Further, if you own assets jointly with your spouse, partner, or other intended beneficiaries (see Chapter 3), you'll avoid probate. Also, many if not most of your assets may never be subject to probate anyway because they pass to heirs without the formal probate process (e.g., retirement assets and insurance pass by beneficiary designations, not probate). Probate should not be the primary focus of your planning. If your estate is modest and there are no major family issues, probate will in most cases not be that big of a deal. Most importantly, planning to minimize probate is no different for someone with a chronic illness and anyone else, so there are few special planning ideas to be provided. Finally, a tremendously powerful tool to protect you from the disabilities and other manifestations of COPD is to use a revocable living trust. There is no more powerful mechanism to protect you through disability. This same technique, the living trust, can easily be used to avoid probate. In fact, this is the most common use of living trusts. Thus, planning to manage your assets during disability may also avoid probate. See Chapter 10.

## ESTATE TAXES

For wealthy taxpayers seeking to minimize estate taxes and who also suffer from COPD, the core of planning and the modifications are similar to those discussed in this book. So even wealthy readers can benefit from all the topics discussed in this book. However, those with large estates will have to layer this book's planning ideas with the tax, asset protection, and other planning typically pursued by wealthy taxpayers. Issues of competency, time frame, management, and so on need to be considered regardless of wealth. The details of actual tax strategies are beyond the scope of this book.

The federal estate tax does not apply in 2012 unless your estate (the net value of all you own) exceeds $5.12 million. This figure is scheduled to decrease to $1 million in 2013, although few tax experts believe this will be allowed by Congress to happen. While it's impossible to determine what changes might occur with the federal estate tax, it's fairly safe to assume that you'd have to be in the wealthiest couple of percent of the country in terms of net worth to have to be concerned. If you have anywhere near that amount of money, you need to hire an estate planning attorney, and you can afford to do so. This book will still give you a lot of information to tailor your customized estate plan to address planning with a chronic illness, but you should not even consider using the sample forms. Too many estate planning books focus on taxes when it is simply not an issue for the vast majority of Americans. Try this statistic on for size. Only 18,431 estates filed estate tax returns with the IRS in 2004. That was less than 1 percent of the estates of all people who died in 2004 (.8 percent, to be exact). In 2012 it was estimated that only about 5,600 estates a year will file a federal estate tax return and pay a federal estate tax. Taxes, while tremendously important for some people, is not relevant to most. But given the uncertainty about the future of the tax laws, confirm the appropriateness of these comments with your attorney.

Thus, for the majority of people with COPD, the estate tax is a separate matter from the real personal issues. Not to say that tax planning isn't important; it is. Income tax issues are significant too. Assets owned on death get a "step up in basis." This means that the cost or investment in those assets is increased to the fair value at death, which can avoid all capital gains tax. Many states have estate or inheritance taxes that begin at much lower levels than the federal amount. But again, if taxes can be an issue, get professional help for all your planning. But whatever you do, don't lose your focus on taking care of yourself and addressing the nuances COPD has on many of your planning documents.

## MEDICAID AND SIMILAR PLANNING

Medicaid is a government program that provides certain benefits to persons with minimal resources. There are many planning issues that those living with chronic illness need to address. In fact, from a financial perspective, qualifying for these programs may be the most important step you can take to secure your financial future. These matters, however, will not be addressed to a significant degree in this book, other than a brief discussion of how they have an impact on provisions your family or loved ones may wish to include in their estate planning documents to protect you. See Chapter 12. Medicaid and similar planning has been addressed in other books and resources available to those living with chronic illness. To address it here would only detract from the focus of this book, and the information contained herein is not available elsewhere. So we'll stay focused on COPD's impact on planning.

## CHAPTER SUMMARY

This chapter has provided an introduction and overview to what the estate planning process is about, and how it must be modified to address the nuances of COPD. In order to protect yourself, estate and financial planning is vital. However, the planning that is "standard" and applicable for the "typical" person simply won't suffice to address many of your needs. The following chapters address each of the important issues and documents you'll need to address estate planning and your special circumstances.

## CHAPTER 3

# Comorbidity, Emotional Considerations, and Competency: Ancillary Issues Critical to Planning for Those Living with COPD

## What Is Comorbidity?

FOR SOMEONE LIVING WITH COPD, planning can be complicated by issues of other health challenges. COPD is often accompanied by comorbid (co-existing) diseases that might include lung infections, diabetes, sleep apnea, cancer, hypertension, cardiovascular disease, and other ailments. Physical complications of COPD present a significant issue for many people. Oxygen deprivation resulting from COPD can lead to organ damage. Heart function and circulation can be impaired. Thus, merely stating that you are living with COPD may not be adequate to understand the full impact of the disease course and its affects on your planning, and, in particular, your present status. Thus, to properly plan you need to explain any other health issues to your planner. These are not generally discussed in this book because of the wide variability of other potential conditions.

In spite of COPD symptoms and even comorbidity, most people living with COPD live relatively normal life spans, into their 70s and 80s. Appropriate medical intervention, rehabilitation, and lifestyle choices can extend both quality of life and life expectancy.

# EMOTIONAL, PSYCHOLOGICAL, AND COMPETENCY ISSUES ARE INTERRELATED

Emotional, psychological, and competency issues for someone living with COPD may be interrelated. While these challenges will be discussed in greater detail below, they are introduced here with a case study.

## ○  COPD Case Study

COPD can result in the destruction of the lungs. Many lay people might view this purely as a physical impairment that should not have a emotional cognitive impact. But is that really the case? COPD can damage self-esteem with the same vengeance that it attacks lung tissue. Tremendous anxiety may occur, even in the early stages of the illness. With COPD, if there is an acute event (e.g., a flare-up), you could become hypoxic and acutely confused. But, after treatment and recovery, when your oxygen levels recover sufficiently, you may revert to your cognitive baseline prior to the event. However, if there are many flare-ups or repeated assaults, some people living with COPD might not fully recover or return to baseline. There may be permanent brain damage. In contrast, others with COPD might experience many flare-ups and not experience any brain damage. Even if you return to a baseline from a cognitive perspective, you may not fully recover from an emotional perspective. If you have experienced repeated flare-ups, it might be advisable to have an assessment done of your mental capacity before signing any significant legal documents. This is especially true if your dispositive scheme is not a natural one (e.g., all to one child, nothing to another, etc.). Anyone in a panic over not breathing will likely be terrified and that is not the time to execute any legal document. If you've recently had an event occur, or remain shaken from a recent one, discuss with your attorney the possible benefits of letting more time pass before signing documents or making any significant decisions. All of this can make planning for someone with COPD far more challenging that perhaps initially anticipated. COPD as a disease appears to be primarily physical. However, it can have profound cognitive and/or emotional impact. Your attorney should be advised to take precautions to ensure that they don't misinterpret your status. If your mobility is limited from the fatigue and breathing issues, this may increase the risk of your being abused or of someone unduly influencing your estate or financial decisions.

# HOW MIGHT EMOTIONAL AND PSYCHOLOGICAL RESPONSES TO COPD AFFECT YOUR PLANNING?

The physical symptoms of COPD can be further exacerbated by a range of emotional and psychological issues. The physical symptoms of COPD—deteriorating lung function, which leads to a reduction in physical abilities and increasing fatigue—and the difficulties these can create can also lead to anxiety. The physical symptoms of COPD frequently lead to depression. If you are affected by depression, getting motivated to address financial and estate planning won't be easy. Most people view the estate planning process as about as enjoyable as a root canal. But in spite of the depression you may face, remember that the lack of planning will potentially weigh heavier on you than on those without your challenges.

Since many of those living with COPD were smokers, there is often an element of guilt associated with the disease that can heighten the depression associated with advancing symptoms. Since COPD for many is caused by smoking, the disease may have been avoidable. This fact can create tremendous guilt and anger that can make the stages the client traverses following diagnosis difficult. But focusing on any of these negative emotions will only cause you further difficulties by delaying or undermining the planning process (worse, it may undermine your seeking the appropriate medical help and diligently following your prescribed medical regimen).

The smoking foundation for many with COPD often translates into a stigmatization of those living with COPD. Many with COPD fear that family and even physicians will blame them for contracting the disease. These psychosocial considerations are rather unique to COPD as contrasted to those living with other chronic diseases. Even if this is true, you are entitled to unbiased professional treatment from any professional advisers you hire. Neither your advisers, medical team, or others have the right to judge you or health issues you did not choose. Significantly, the stigmatization is inappropriate. The reality is that only 20% of those who smoke ultimately develop significant COPD. This suggests that other factors, genetic and environmental, must contribute to the onset of the disease. Heart disease, diabetes, and obesity do not tend to have the stigmatization that COPD does.

An unfortunate result of these misconceptions is that many people living with COPD don't explain their condition and its impact to their advisers. The result is that estate planning attorneys, CPAs, and financial planners may not ascertain whether you have a health issue that may affect planning. If you yourself are in denial, you might not reveal critical information. No planner can execute his or her responsibilities for a client with COPD if the planner does not know that the client is living with COPD. If you are struggling to deal with these issues, seek help. Your primary care physician can recommend a social worker, care manager, psychologist, or psychiatrist to help you. The real tragedy will be that if you don't address your planning, your medical challenges will be compounded by financial and legal dilemmas. Take charge and help yourself.

There is another approach you might consider. If depression or other personal factors prove a significant impediment to your undertaking or completing planning, consider giving your attorney, CPA, and wealth manager permission to communicate with designated loved ones or family members to enlist their help in coaxing you forward in the planning process. For your attorney to speak with anyone but you about your matters they must have your express permission or the "attorney client privilege" will prevent such communications. Your discussions with your lawyer must remain confidential unless you authorize your attorney to discuss them with others. Accountants also have a host of restrictions that they may face, so they might need written approvals as well. Depending on your situation (perhaps especially if you were recently diagnosed), it may be advisable to authorize your planning team to communicate with family or others. If you face a worsening cognitive condition, this may be essential. However, for COPD the communication may more likely be to address the above concerns. Here's illustrative language your advisers might use:

> "I expressly authorize ATTORNEY NAME to communicate with the agent named under my durable power of attorney, health care proxy, as well as my wealth manager ADVISORY FIRM NAME, and my Certified Public Accountant CPA FIRM NAME. Collectively my agents and named professional advisers, and the successors to those advisory firms, are collectively referred to as 'Recipients.' I understand that ATTORNEY NAME will have to exercise judgment as to what communication is appropriate in the circumstances. Therefore, I authorize ATTORNEY NAME in their sole discretion

to communicate, or not communicate, with any person named as a Recipient, or any successor or alternate to them. I understand and agree that this authorization constitutes an express waiver of the attorney-client privilege which I have with ATTORNEY NAME. I, on behalf of myself and my estate, guardian, committee or successors and assigns, hold ATTORNEY NAME harmless from the exercise or non-exercise of this power."

# USING A CARE MANAGER TO HELP YOU AND YOUR LOVED ONES ADDRESS EMOTIONAL AND PSYCHOLOGICAL RESPONSES TO COPD

Addressing the wide range of medical and personal decisions, coordinating a daunting care plan, addressing psychosocial issues, and communicating this information to your estate planning team can be a challenge, but for many an impossible task. A care manager can assist you with each of these tasks. A care manager can also help you through this grieving process of an initial diagnosis, help you accept the challenges of living with COPD, as well as address new issues of grief as the disease progresses. They can help you to redefine yourself and either adapt future plans or set new goals to accommodate living with a chronic illness.

It is important to note that the presence of a chronic illness like COPD should not be about what you as a person "can't do," but rather what you can still do. A well-done estate and financial plan can protect and empower you too. And that should be the goal.

Care managers can work with you to build the plan of care for the issues that may arise with your particular diagnosis. Beginning with the nursing diagnosis, your care manager may utilize nursing or other skills in performing an assessment of you, assisting you in planning and implementation, and so on. The care manager will hopefully be able to involve you in your plan of care, and help you begin to take a positive perspective in addressing current concerns. This approach may empower you and help you to focus on your abilities. This further helps you maintain a sense of control over your life and future. This can serve to facilitate the entire financial and estate planning process. But for this intervention, many people, especially the newly diagnosed, may not proceed with the planning. Care managers can encourage you to work with a financial planner and provide you with recommendations for care that allow you and your planners the information necessary to create an overall plan that is best for you. The involvement of a care manager as part of the estate planning team can prove to be invaluable in addressing the current and long-term financial-related care needs after your diagnosis.

## WHAT IS COMPETENCY?

Competency is a legal concept, not a psychological or medical concept. As illustrated in the case study earlier in this chapter, while many people assume COPD solely has a physical impact, it can have a significant emotional or psychological effect; it can even affect competency.

In terms of estate planning, competency can come down to having to convince a judge or jury that a particular document in question (e.g., a will, trust, power of attorney) is a fair expression of your reasonably healthy judgment. Your attorney may be required to prove that you should not be declared incompetent.

Many people mistakenly believe competency is purely a medical concept, when in fact competency is really a legal determination. Your lawyer, not only your physician, will have to be involved in the process of ultimately determining whether you are legally competent. People assume a single or uniform definition exists for competency. In fact, there are a host of different definitions under different situations. The law recognizes various incarnations of the term "competency": The degree of competency to sign a will (called "testamentary capacity") is less than that required to execute a contract (called "contractual capacity").

The circumstances of the specific matter weigh on how competency in that situation should be assessed. Assessing competency is a function of what degree of capacity a specific legal action requires. The more complex the matter, the greater the degree of competency required.

The timing of the determination as to whether you were competent is quite important. The question in many competency challenges is not "whether" you were incompetent, but "when" you became incompetent. With COPD you may have, as illustrated above, significant confusion or anxiety following a flare-up. But are those effects permanent? Did you recover to baseline? If you did, at what point in time? Did a home health aide cajole you into signing a new will naming her as a beneficiary while you were still affected in the aftermath of an acute attack? Or were you actually at the time quite lucid and seeking to thank a long-time health aide who has loyally served you when family abandoned you?

Establishing with some specificity at what point in the time continuum your competency waned, or when you lapsed into incompetence, or if and when and to what degree you recovered, is often problematic and can often be center of a legal challenge. If you signed an estate planning document while deemed competent, the contractual arrangement should be respected. If you were not capable of understanding the transaction, the IRS or an heir may overturn the arrangement. For example, if you wanted to favor your son who took regular care of you during your illness and provide a lesser bequest to your daughter who was seemingly indifferent to your health struggles, the issue of your competency to do so could be critical (see Chapter 12).

Determining your level of capacity is vital in order to ascertain what actions may be appropriately taken. If your attorney has more than a mild question as to your competency, he or she will likely evaluate the need for you to have a formal competency assessment. This could entail having your attending physician provide an evaluation of your physical condition with an emphasis on how it may have an impact on your competency, your neurologist or psychiatrist providing an evaluation of your mental capacity, your pulmonologist addressing the status of your COPD and the history of any attacks, and your attorney making a final conclusion as to competency.

## TESTAMENTARY CAPACITY

Testamentary capacity refers to whether you have the competence to sign a will. This requires that you know the natural objects of your bounty (children, grandchildren, etc.), understand the nature and extent of your property (what assets you own, your balance sheet), and the relationship of both to make a rational distribution in your will. Some definitions require that you have sufficient mind and memory and be capable of understanding the general nature of the matter in which you are engaged, namely, making a will. You should also understand the interrelationship of these factors. Capacity is required only when your will is executed, so that the will is executed during a lucid interval, and your attorney must be able to demonstrate that this in fact occurred. You can be incapacitated before and after the execution with no legal consequences. The level of capacity that you must have to execute a will is relatively low and less than the requisite capacity to execute the contractual documents often included in an estate and financial plan. A person may, in fact, execute a will even if classified by his or her physician as insane, feeble-minded, a drug addict, and even suffering at times from a partial loss of memory related to persons and things.

What might this all mean to you if you are living with COPD? If someone is challenging your will, that person might try to prove you signed your will near the time of an acute event (e.g., a flare-up) and that you might have been anxious or confused as a result. If you have severe COPD, he or she might argue you were not competent.

Bear in mind that testamentary capacity is the lowest level of competency and many, perhaps most, of your assets may be controlled by beneficiary designations (e.g., IRA, insurance, etc.). Those require a higher level of capacity.

## CONTRACTUAL CAPACITY

This refers to the competency you must have to sign a contract. For you to have contractual capacity, you must generally understand the nature and effect of the act and the business being transacted. If the business being transacted is highly complicated, a higher level of understanding may be needed. Having sufficient capacity to execute a will does not demonstrate your capacity to sign or enter into a contract, because a greater degree of capacity is necessary to understand this more complex transaction. For many business documents (e.g., partnership agreement), the document itself may include its own definition of disability, including issues of competency. In such instances, you or your attorney needs to review the governing legal document. The threshold level of competency for you to retain shares and a directorship in a closely held business may be much more stringent than the level of competency that is required to contract in general.

## POWER OF ATTORNEY

A power of attorney is a document in which you designate a person (agent) to handle your financial affairs if you can't (see Chapter 5). The capacity required to execute a power of attorney varies by jurisdiction. In some states, only capacity similar to that required to sign a will (testamentary capacity) is required. In others, the capacity to contract is required.

### LIVING WILL AND HEALTH PROXY

These are documents used to address your health care decisions (see Chapter 8). Capacity to execute these documents is tied to the legal doctrine of informed consent. A patient has the right to control contact with his or her person. Informed consent to such contact requires that the patient provide voluntary, competent, and informed consent. Although some courts have held that the capacity to provide informed consent is similar to the capacity required to contract, the law in this regard is not clear and clinical models of capacity are therefore often used instead.

## WHY COMPETENCY MATTERS

Determining competency is a critical issue for many estate plans, as well as many tax audits. Competency is the prerequisite to the validity of any estate plan, but remains widely misunderstood. If you are not competent, then any document you sign or any transaction you complete will be ineffectual. That's significant. Unfortunately, what constitutes competency varies by the circumstances. The trend of our aging population raises more and more questions about issues of competency, and these will be raised with more frequency over time. Furthermore, the ever-growing pharmacopeia of treatments for diseases that afflict the elderly resulting in lengthened life span will bring even more complexity to the competency analysis.

## COPD AND COMPETENCY MISCONCEPTIONS

There are many misconceptions about competency, especially with respect to people with chronic illness. Some people, for example, assume that anyone with a chronic illness has significant competency issues. While some chronic illnesses do result in dementia, like Alzheimer's disease, many, such as COPD, generally do not. While it is true that many people with COPD may need assistance with their financial and legal affairs because of the stress or physical strenuousness of handling certain matters, this does not imply the existence of any cognitive issues. However, severe COPD has been associated with lower cognitive function in older adults. Those living with COPD may experience periods of low oxygen levels (called "hypoxia") that might lead to brain abnormalities that could reduce cognitive capacity. The use of home oxygen may reduce this potential. In some of the studies, the Folstein Mini-Mental State Exam (MMSE) was used to measure cognitive impact.

If your will is challenged, a jury might well have the same misconceptions about your cognition. Those seeking to overturn any legal document you signed might look at your history and argue that oxygen deprivation had an impact. It is therefore important that your estate planner and other professionals are adequately versed on what constitutes mental incapacity and what does not, and especially the impact that COPD may or may not have. Some simple and inexpensive steps like corroborating that your competency has not been materially compromised by oxygen deprivation (e.g., from the regular use of home oxygen as documented in periodic care manager reports), that flare-ups or acute events have not occurred, or that if they did, that there was no cognitive impact based on medical records, and other steps may deflect a will challenge or other legal challenge.

KEY

> **You must communicate in clear detail to all your advisers what your current cognitive situation is, whether it will likely decline, and over what approximate time period.**

# COPD and Cognitive Issues

### DECLINING COGNITIVE ABILITY

A deterioration in cognitive function is often defined in terms of a decline in memory accompanied by other cognitive impairments. Cognitive decline has a host of implications to the estate planning process:

❖ It creates a sense of urgency to complete planning while feasible.

❖ It determines and corroborates whether you are competent to complete a particular plan or to sign a particular document.

❖ It signals the need for planning for potentially long-term disability.

If you are living with severe COPD, act to complete planning and documents while you are able to do so.

# WHAT YOUR ESTATE PLANNER SHOULD KNOW AND DO

There are a number of points your estate planner should consider in helping you. You might want to discuss this list with your planner:

❖     Don't make assumptions.

❖     Understand that there is tremendous variability among those living with COPD, but particular caution must be used if you have severe COPD. Even more confusing, there can be significant variability in the cognitive impact experienced at different times by the same client. If a meeting occurs shortly after an acute event, there may or may not have been a full recovery. So in contrast to a disease like Alzheimer's for which a continued decline in cognitive ability is assured, a patient with COPD may actually have recovery of cognitive ability after an attack.

❖     Whether or not you have had any negative cognitive impact because of COPD, the risk of oxygen deprivation causing a problem in the future should not be ignored. Therefore, planning should not be deferred for long.

❖     When implementing estate and tax planning, consideration should be given to corroborating your competency to avoid challenges at a later date. This should be done even if you have no significant cognitive impairment, given the ignorance of so many people about the effects of chronic illness generally, and especially about the cognitive affects of COPD.

❖     You may have the mental capacity to sign a will (called "testamentary capacity"), but may not have the capacity to engage in more complex contractual transactions, such as a sale of a family business interest to a defective grantor dynasty trust.

❖     Your assets should be consolidated and simplified. It is easier when living with COPD, especially with the potential for worsening physical or cognitive challenges, to interact with a single integrated wealth manager than with a half-dozen or more banks, brokerage firms, and other investment professionals.

❖     Follow meetings and substantive phone conversations with an action list of prioritized bullet points that you must address. This should not be a multiple page memo, but a concise and clear bullet list of items.

❖     Break the planning process into distinct phases, each to be accomplished sequentially to facilitate completing the process in a manner that is easier for you. For example, Phase I might be to complete powers of attorney, living wills, HIPAA releases, and health proxies. Phase II might be to complete a revocable living trust and will. Phase III might address beneficiary designations and trusts. More sophisticated planning might be handled as Phase IV. Discrete, logically organized, and sequential steps will be much easier.

❖     Request that your loved ones or caregiver observe your conduct for signs of diminished capacity, paying attention to factors that suggest change. These might include comments from other friends or family members. You might (and should) raise the issue yourself if you can.

❖     Consider whether a Folstein MMSE may be administered periodically, perhaps by a care manager, as a means of documenting your status. This entails responding to a series of questions and performing certain actions, all of which are scored. The range of scores provides an indication of normal, borderline, or impaired capacity. There are a host of other screening methodologies that can be used.

❖     Assess the degree of physical, financial, or other harm to you from the transaction involved. For example, giving a caregiver a power of attorney to control your financial assets is far riskier than signing a will that divides an estate equally among your natural children.

❖     Analyze your ability to articulate the reasoning leading to a decision, your ability to understand the consequences of that decision, and whether the decision is consistent with your long-term goals and values. Your advisers' retention of meeting notes to demonstrate a consistent pattern of thought and planning may support your ability to make a particular testamentary disposition.

❖     Weigh what documents are being signed, the complexity of the documents overall (the big picture), and any other relevant circumstances.

❖     Document observations of your capacity as well as observations of other professionals involved. For example, two lawyers in the firm each meet separately with you for interviews and each independently documents discussions and observations.

❖    If you have very severe COPD that is likely to progress to the point where a guardian or conservator may be necessary, your attorney should advise you to designate the person and successors that you would want to serve as guardian while you are competent to do so. Many states will permit this.

❖    If your capacity has diminished to the point where new documents cannot be signed, then efforts should be directed to reviewing and implementing existing documents and planning, regardless of their shortcomings. Often planning goals can be achieved even with inadequate existing documents through creative use of title to assets, interpretations or permitted modifications of existing documents, or court intervention.

❖    Your attorney should question whether your actions are rational, expected, and appropriate. For example, have you selected an appropriate beneficiary (one or more of your children) or made a choice that might be considered aberrational (e.g., leaving everything to your health aide)? It is much easier to prove that "normal" behavior is acting in a manner that benefits your children rather then a home health aide. If your attorney must one day address your decision when establishing your competency, the latter choice might be evidence that you did something contrary to what normal expectation would be and might raise questions about other decisions you made while ill.

❖    Obtain appropriate physician letters, attesting to your physical and mental status and indicating any medical issues that may have an impact on your cognitive functions. For example, it may be helpful to have a letter from your pulmonologist confirming that there have been no identifiable acute events that would have had an impact on competency, a letter from your internist stating that there are no other medical issues (comorbidity) that might impair your cognitive capacity. However, this letter must be precise to be of any value. If vague terms like "normal" or phrases like "patient has excellent judgment" are used, what do they mean? Without clear and defined terms, a letter from an attending physician may have little relevance. The physician letter should provide details of the examination given, your current medical condition, the results of a current physical examination, whether there are medical issues that require further inquiry (e.g., unexplained symptoms or symptoms that might be explained by a serious disability that may affect cognition), a psychosocial history, a description of your current living circumstances, and so on. The physician letter should also confirm that you were questioned about people, places, and time. The questions and your responses should be documented.

❖ Make documents understandable. This is quite a challenge when dealing with tax complexities and other complicated matters. No court or jury will believe that you understood a document if they cannot understand it. If a jury cannot understand what your will or other documents intend, they are likely to suspect your competency to sign it. Documents must be sufficiently clear, with consideration to the unavoidable complexity of tax and other laws, so that the average person can understand them. Anything that makes a document intelligible to a layperson is helpful. Often all this requires is a simple, explanatory, and lead-in sentence. When the complexity necessitated by tax laws, property laws (e.g., rule against perpetuities), asset protection, and other steps makes a simple document an impossibility, your attorney might endeavor to make it easier to comprehend with captions or other devices that make the information simpler.

❖ "To videotape or not to videotape." If William Shakespeare, Esq., had been an estate planner, that would have been the question. If your lawyer records you signing a will, certain conditions must be observed. First, you must state your intention regarding the distribution of property and that it is your wish that the will not be challenged. This should be done as you look right into the camera as talking directly to the judge or jury. If, however, you know that the video will not support your competency (e.g., because of your weak appearance), your attorney should not attempt to videotape your will signing.

❖ If a clinical evaluation must be made as to your competency, your attorney should select the appropriate clinician to undertake the analysis. In many cases, this would be a mental health professional who is knowledgeable about the specific health problems you face (e.g., a pulmonologist with expertise in COPD and oxygen deprivation), familiar with the various assessment approaches relevant to the issue of determining capacity in relation to your illness, and with considerable experience conducting competency evaluations.

❖    Your attorney should then take appropriate actions in response to the above findings and determine what steps should be taken to protect you. For example, if you are competent but have progressing severe COPD that may lessen capacity over time, your attorney should help you update all documents and planning, review in detail a durable power of attorney, and take other steps.

## ADDITIONAL POINTS TO CONSIDER

Your family or loved ones will need a formal signed HIPAA (Health Insurance Portability and Accountability Act of 1996) release to obtain medical records. It may, in fact, be advisable to obtain the release and medical records early in the process. Not only will this support the planning process, but it can be significantly easier to do so while you are functioning at your best, rather than at a later date when you may no longer be able or willing to sign the release.

Your attorney should consider constructing a time line of events, including ancillary or tangential matters. Often a time line can truly tell a story demonstrating competency. The major points on the time line would be psychological examinations finding competency, physician letters attesting to competency or the lack of known physical conditions likely to negatively impact cognition, execution of a will or other legal documents where counsel and witnesses can attest to competency, and so on. However, anecdotal evidence can also help tell the story you need.

### EXAMPLE

If you are admitted to the hospital and discharged, what do the examinations prior to discharge indicate? Were the predischarge examinations really relevant to competency? Even an examination by a neurologist may be of little or modest relevance depending on the purpose and nature of the examination. Often a discharge summary may exist in the patient record. It may include comments such as "AOx3" (alert and oriented in all three spheres), a potentially positive and telling sign. But look beyond these significant events at other matters as well. What, for example, did the nursing notes say? Often these notes will describe a patient's conduct and behavior, something that may support competency or underscore cognitive impairment.

## Chapter Summary

Competency is the threshold issue to address in all planning. Because the degree of cognitive impact of COPD can be quite different for different patients, and can change over time, this must be addressed for everyone living with COPD when pursuing planning.

## CHAPTER 4

# ORGANIZING LEGAL, FINANCIAL, AND OTHER INFORMATION

## THE KEY TO YOUR SECURITY

## WHY IT IS VITAL TO ORGANIZE YOUR INFORMATION

IF YOU DON'T KNOW WHAT YOU HAVE, you cannot plan for it. Pretty simple and straightforward. Everyone undertaking estate and financial planning needs to start by organizing all of their legal, financial, tax, and other important information. Organization is essential to your proper investment planning, ensuring appropriate insurance coverage, optimal ownership (titling) of assets, and determining what type of estate planning documents you need. When living with COPD, the stress of disorganization or financial or legal problems can tax your abilities, or even worsen a flare-up. Organization of your records and documents is essential. Consider:

❖    Your will governs only those assets that pass through your estate (probate). If you have a brokerage account that is POD (pay on death) to a niece, it will pass automatically to her on your death. Your will is irrelevant. Accurate financial data are essential to determine how your assets will be distributed at death. Filling in a cheap will on an Internet site won't provide you with this type of guidance.

❖    Making sure you have proper property and casualty insurance requires an understanding of what assets you have.

❖    A durable power of attorney, an essential document for everyone (especially someone with a COPD), is of limited practical use if your agent doesn't have the necessary information to act.

❖     A revocable living trust is the most powerful estate and financial planning tool to protect you. But to gain the optimal benefit of this tool, you and your advisers have to identify which assets can, and which cannot, be transferred to your living trust.

Because you have a chronic illness, this step takes on even greater importance than it does for others. And as your disease progresses it becomes even more important. No matter what your prognosis, it is more likely that a time will come when you are unable to complete all necessary tasks yourself and will require the assistance of others. You want to be hyperorganized and keep all your records as simple as possible. The old KISS principle (keep it simple, stupid) should be your goal. If your disease may cause cognitive symptoms, you may one day reach a point where you will not be able to instruct people what to do and how to act or give them pertinent information. Organizing everything before that point will ensure an easier time for all concerned. Even if your disease course never presents cognitive symptoms, you may become homebound, hospitalized, or may require surgery, during which you are unable to perform these tasks yourself. By systematically categorizing and labeling all important documents, you can make attending to your needs a simple task for your agent and your loved ones who help out.

❖     The more organized your documents and finances are, the easier it will be for you to retain as much control yourself, as long as possible. If you can consolidate all your financial assets into one institution, preferably with a single master statement for all of your accounts, they will be easier to monitor, especially if you experience cognitive issues.

❖     If your affairs are clear, simple, and organized, you can remain involved and in control to the maximum extent possible, turning over the portions of your finances you need help with incrementally, rather than all at one time.

❖     Depending on how your illness progresses, you may eventually need someone to take over portions of the financial and administrative work. The easier, more organized, and more automatic, the better that person will do. This will allow your agent to spend the most time working on what you need, not scrambling to find important documents.

❖     Organization will create an easily identifiable history of what you've done in the past. This can provide valuable guidance for those helping you if at some future point you cannot communicate your wishes. For example, a computerized checkbook will point out your pattern of gifts, charitable donations, and so on. It will also facilitate your transition to handling as many matters as possible online without the added strain of having to physically go to a bank or post office.

## How to Organize Your Information

The best way to organize most of your records and documents is electronically. But using the analogy of physical organization tools will help best understand the electronic organization. Also, there are many documents that you will still want to keep in physical format.

A simple and effective way to organize your important documents and information is to set up a primary loose-leaf binder in which you will store most, if not all, of your documents. You may prefer a system of coded file folders, perhaps in a rolling bin to hold them. The advantage of a binder over folders is that papers won't fall out and get lost. Another approach is an accordion file sold in office supply stores. Figure out what works best for you, and if the approach you've chosen becomes impractical or difficult, you can always change.

Whatever filing system you use, the next step is to create tabs and label them for each of the categories of documents contained in your primary binder. Taking some time to plan out how you will organize your financial and legal documents is important. You want a simple approach that makes it readily obvious what is filed where to anyone coming in to help you. As your cognitive abilities decline, it will be easier to stay on top of everything. Color coding (e.g., tabs for legal documents in blue, assets in green, liabilities and credit cards in red, etc.) can help too. If you have a complex situation with respect to a particular tab/category, you need to set up a separate supplemental loose-leaf binder for those documents. Depending on your situation, you may need to use one or more supplementary loose-leaf binders in addition to your primary binder.

EXAMPLE

Let's assume you have a home-based business. In your primary binder, you might include summary data on the business and indicate that there is a separate binder or folder system for the business. This way, you can break out the business documents and finances with appropriate detail to be helpful to you or someone helping you without cluttering your general finances and legal records.

These properly organized binders (folders or other files) are necessary to identify the planning steps that can improve your legal, tax, or financial situation. Any time you set up a supplementary binder to handle paperwork in a particular area, be sure to reference that supplemental binder in your primary binder. Thus, any heir, agent, business partner, and so on, will be directed to the additional information.

These are possible sections to consider when organizing your filing system. If one does not apply, you may omit it. Add additional components or sections that might make sense for you.

1. Contents
2. Emergency
3. Basic background information
4. Medical and health information
5. Banking and financial information
6. Credit cards and liabilities
7. Securities and other investments
8. Insurance information
9. Estate planning documents
10. Tax information
11. Business interests
12. Personal property
13. Real estate records
14. Retirement asset information
15. Miscellaneous assets
16. Wallet
17. Budgeting

EXAMPLE

There are very powerful software packages that can help you organize almost everything you can think of. As an example, a product called CareBinders®

organizes and stores individual, family, and even small business documents all in one place, fully secure, residing right on your personal computer. It tracks personal, medical, financial and small business data of all kinds for each family member. Data, reports, and attachments are easily backed up onto a flash drive and even onto your mobile device for portability. They even offer a "JumpStart" concierge service for people who want to get organized but find the task a daunting one. See www.cbdatasystems.com. Once everything is organized electronically, trusted family or friends can use an Internet service like GoToMeeting or LogMein to review your data on your computer from wherever they are.

## WHERE TO KEEP YOUR PHYSICAL RECORDS, DOCUMENTS, AND INFORMATION

Once you have assembled and organized your documents into a binder or folder system, you need to decide where to place them so they can be easily reached in an emergency. If you have a filing cabinet or a home office, it may be a good idea to store your binder there, since it will probably be the first place someone will look. It is also important to inform your agents, spouse, and other loved ones about the location of your documents, so they have easy access to everything in case of an emergency. Keep in mind that if your disease includes cognitive symptoms, this system may also be designed to assist you as your disease progresses. So keep your binder somewhere that is easily accessible and logical for you (i.e., in a place you usually keep things of this kind, not hidden in some location you seldom use or see). A fireproof file cabinet might be an ideal location.

## COMPUTERIZE YOUR FINANCES

One of the most productive things you can do is to computerize your finances and related matters. The cost of computers has declined dramatically over the years, while the capabilities have increased. The most significant benefit of computerization is that you can automate many tasks, which makes it safer and easier for you to keep in control of your affairs longer. Here are some of the ways computerization can help:

❖　If your checkbook and investment accounts are computerized (see quicken.intuit.com), you can use a large screen to magnify text or have voice software to make it easier to deal with documents.

❖    You can easily back up to a thumb drive, CD, or DVD to store off site or, better yet, use an online backup service that will automatically back up your data over the Internet regularly. See www.sugarsync.com. The more you automate, the easier it is to manage. The more you automate the less stress you'll have over finding information, missing an important payment, and so on.

❖    You can set up automatic monthly bill paying and reminders for other clerical tasks, such as checking your free credit report from one of the three main credit agencies every four months, and so on.

❖    Online bill payments can help you avoid many tasks that are or may become difficult as a result of fatigue or other issues. No more envelopes, stamps, and so forth. This means you can avoid the envelope stuffing, and even more importantly, trips to banks and other locations that may be difficult for you or potentially dangerous depending on weather conditions.

❖    You can easily back up selected data to give to your accountant to help you with tax planning or returns. If you want to save money and your returns are simple, it's easy to import your data from a computerized checkbook (like Quicken) into a tax preparation program (like TurboTax) and do returns on your own. That not only can be a huge money saver, but it also eliminates additional efforts involved in dealing with an outside accountant. However, if your situation is complex or you have a business, spend the money and make the effort to use a qualified CPA. A CPA can also be a great resource overall, so weigh the loss of that benefit.

❖    Budgeting is essential to investment, financial, and estate planning. (If you run out of money your will won't be of much use!) Most computerized checkbook and financial programs have simple, powerful, and easy to use budgeting functions. The reports that you can easily print and use will help you complete most of the important budgeting steps. In addition, if you maintain your personal checkbook and financial account records in such a program, a printout of your net worth statement (or perhaps a balance sheet if you operate a business) will be a helpful add-on to your documents. This report will also include much of the data your estate planner needs.

Every effort you make to organize documents will pay you dividends of less stress, more secure financial status, and easier management of your affairs as COPD or even just age, make these tasks more difficult.

# WHAT INFORMATION TO ORGANIZE

## ESTATE PLANNING DOCUMENTS

Once you've finalized and signed all the appropriate documents discussed in this book, you need to organize them to make them accessible to those who will help you. You should sign only one original will. Depending on what your attorney advises, you might sign only one, or perhaps three or more originals of certain of the other documents. Multiple originals (but not your will) can enable you to retain an original of each, with other signed originals being given to your agent or other fiduciary (e.g., trustee), and perhaps your lawyer. Below is a breakdown of where documents can be kept. In any event, you should keep a photocopy behind a tab (or in a file) labeled "Estate Planning Documents." If your original is in your safe deposit box, safe, etc., you can note on your copy where the original is kept. The cost of home copier/scanners/printers has become so inexpensive that everyone should invest the money and time to scan all critical documents and records.

❖ *Power of attorney.* Give an original to the first agent (person named in the power to help you with your financial and legal matters), a copy to each successor agent (the agents who serve if your first agent can't), and keep an original with your personal papers. You might also give a copy to your financial planner (wealth manager).

❖ *Living will.* Give an original to the first agent (person named in the power to help with your health care decisions if you cannot), a copy to each successor agent (the agents who serve if your first agent can't), and keep an original with your personal papers. You might also give a copy to your attending physicians (e.g., your internist and neurologist) to include in your chart.

❖ *HIPAA release.* Give an original to the first agent (person named in the power to help with monitoring your medical issues), and keep an original with your personal papers. You might also give an original to your attending physician(s) to include in your chart.

❖ *Health care proxy.* Give an original to the first agent (person named in the power to help with your health care decisions if you cannot), a copy to each successor agent (the agents who serve if your first agent can't), and give an original to your lawyer. You might also give a copy to each attending physician and specifically request that it be added to your medical records.

❖     *Will.* In some cases, your lawyer might hold your original will, but many now recommend that their clients retain their own original documents. If your lawyer will hold the original, you should also specifically inquire as to what steps your lawyer will take to safeguard your original will. Does the attorney hold it in a fireproof box (e.g., fire-rated safe or bank safe deposit box)? How does the attorney track original wills? If the attorney is a sole practitioner, what happens if he or she dies? You should have a copy. If you retain the original you should take similar safeguards as recommended for an attorney. Whether you give your executor (and successor executor) a copy depends on the circumstances. You may not want to distribute copies of your will in case your feelings change and you want to change who inherits your assets.

❖     *Living trust.* If you sign only one original living trust, you might want your lawyer to hold it in safekeeping along with your will. Alternatively, you might keep the original and give photocopies to your lawyer and cotrustee. It's also advisable to give copies to your successor trustees as they will be responsible for your protection and for managing your finances if your health deteriorates to the point that you cannot serve, or if the other current trustees cannot serve. If they have a copy of the trust document in advance and are aware of their responsibilities, the transition from the current to the successor trustees will be smoother. Your accountant may want a copy of the trust for the permanent files that accountants typically maintain for clients. Finally, your bank and investment manager may want copies to open up trust bank and brokerage accounts.

## OTHER LEGAL RECORDS

There are a number of other important legal documents for which you may want to organize tabs in your filing system. The following is a listing of some of the most common, with a brief explanation of how and why you might need them for your estate planning. As with estate planning documents, it is recommended that you scan a copy of each of these documents and make sure your computer is backed up regularly through an Internet back-up service.

❖     *Deed.* Your home may be your largest asset, so the legal document that confirms your ownership is important. You might keep a copy of the deed behind the tab (or in a file) labeled "House." You might also keep a copy of the title insurance policy (insurance of your ownership of the house) and other important records in the same location. The deed is vital for your estate planner as verification of how your house is owned (titled). It is essential to your plan that the ownership of your home be consistent with your other planning.

❖    *Divorce agreement.* If you're divorced, a copy of the agreement, and any ancillary documents (e.g., you might have a settlement agreement, a court decree, etc.) should be kept together. These documents are essential for your financial and estate planning as they may indicate important cash flow (e.g., alimony, child support) obligations you may have. There may also be important information related to assets shared with your ex-spouse. For example, your ex-spouse might own half of your house, or you may own half of the house your ex-spouse resides in. These facts are essential for your planners to know. Furthermore, after assembling all the relevant documents, you may want to make some notations as to how you've dealt with issues or responsibilities of the divorce; these can be invaluable to an agent or other fiduciary trying to help you.

❖    *Business documents.* The documents filed to set up your business should be safely stored. These might include a Certificate filed with the state to form your business entity, a shareholders' agreement, and so on.

## FINANCIAL RECORDS

❖    *Life insurance policies.* If you own any insurance, you'll likely want to keep it in force, especially if you purchased it before you were diagnosed with COPD. Details on the policy are vital for a host of reasons. The policy should be periodically reviewed to make certain that it is performing as anticipated, and to determine if there are any options under the policy you should take advantage of. For example, let's say you purchased a term policy prior to your diagnosis; if the policy has a conversion option permitting you to convert the policy to a permanent policy that will never lapse, that could be an economically prudent opportunity that should be addressed. If you have difficulty paying increased premiums, you might be able to borrow funds on the policy, or sell of the policy. Your estate planner will need your insurance information to review whether you should establish a trust to own the policy (generally not the revocable living trust discussed in this book, but rather an irrevocable life insurance trust).

❖     *Brokerage statements, bank statements,* and so forth. You need the data on your various accounts to assemble the balance sheet your lawyer and other planners need. The manner in which those accounts are owned (titled) is also vital to share with these individuals. If the account is joint, the joint owner might automatically obtain ownership of the account on your death. If the account has a beneficiary designation, your planners need to have a copy, as your designation may determine who will inherit the account.

❖     *Retirement accounts.* Copies of account statements, beneficiary designations, plan summary documents (if available), and so on, should be filed behind a tab labeled "Retirement Plans."

❖     *Disability and long-term care insurance coverage.* Copies of any policies should be kept. If you have not reviewed them with a professional since you were diagnosed, you should do so.

## PERSONAL AND FAMILY RECORDS

The following family records are important to assemble:

❖     Listing of key family members, including parents, siblings, spouse, children, and grandchildren. Provide address, age, and other relevant data for each person listed, and note whether anyone on your list is deceased or divorced. Note any additional information you consider significant.

❖     Birth certificate

❖     Marriage certificate

❖     Other key documents

## MEDICAL RECORDS

You should include key medical data in your primary binder and then set up a separate binder that has all pertinent information concerning your health care, particularly with respect to your illness and the unique issues you have to cope with:

❖     Medical and health insurance

❖     Long-term care insurance

❖     General medical information

❖   Nutrition, diet, and related information

❖   Medications

❖   Psychological information

❖   Pulmonologist

❖   Internist

❖   X-rays

❖   Lab reports—arterial blood gas, spirometry, ventilation profusion scan

❖   Travel data and resources

### EMERGENCY INFORMATION

A listing of important names, phone numbers, account numbers, and other data that you or someone helping you can quickly find. This should be the first file or tab in your primary binder.

## PROFESSIONALS YOU MAY USE TO ORGANIZE AND PLAN

To have these issues addressed properly, you need an attorney who devotes a substantial part of his or her practice to nothing but estate planning. You may also want to hire a financial planner in addition to any accountants or insurance agents you already retain. Your planning will benefit greatly from consulting with all of these professionals, and you may want to meet with all of them at the same time, thus allowing them (and you) to discuss your estate plan together. Utilizing all of your professionals to the best of their abilities will greatly benefit your estate. If you cannot afford all these professionals, there are ways to more cost-effectively acheive similar results discussed throughout this book.

## SAMPLE FORMS TO ORGANIZE YOUR RECORDS

Scores of free forms to use in organizing your various financial, legal, and other records can be obtained from www.laweasy.com

## Chapter Summary

This chapter has provided guidance and suggestions for organizing your financial, estate, legal, and other documents. Once these documents are organized, copies of certain documents need to be disseminated to the people you will be relying on. Finally, you need to use the information you have assembled as part of your estate planning process.

## CHAPTER 5

# FINANCIAL PLANNING: THE FOUNDATION OF ANY ESTATE PLAN

## GETTING YOUR FINANCIAL HOUSE IN ORDER

## INTRODUCTION TO FINANCIAL PLANNING FOR COPD

FINANCIAL PLANNING IS A CRITICAL STEP to take in preparing any estate plan. It should be the foundation or backdrop against which all estate planning is addressed. Here's just a few thoughts:

❖ A key document everyone over age 18 should sign, and absolutely anyone living with COPD, is a durable power of attorney to authorize a named person to handle financial, legal, and other matters if you cannot do so. Imposing this tremendous responsibility on family or friends is significant. If your financial house is not in order you'll be adding tremendously to their burden. Signing a legal document without addressing your finances really can't provide the protection you want.

❖ If you don't have a budget, financial plan, and investment plan (and they really should be done in that order as each builds on the other) will you have any money left in your later years for an agent to help you with? Will you have any money left to bequeath in a will?

❖ If your estate is more substantial, can you afford to make large gifts now to help loved ones? You need a financial foundation to make this decision.

❖ The estate tax laws have been in a state of tremendous flux for years. Can you or should you plan? You need the basis of a financial plan to determine what, if anything, you should do.

❖     If your COPD progresses to the point that you will need help, what guidance and framework will you be able to provide those endeavoring to help? Will you have years of easily accessible and well-organized records to provide them detailed guidance on what you would want?

❖     If you were just diagnosed with COPD, how might you change your budget and investment plan today? What misconceptions might your financial planner have that could be detrimental to your financial well-being?

This chapter will barely scratch the surface of these vital issues. The purpose, as noted elsewhere in this book, is to make sure you, the reader, understand how integral financial and investment planning is to the estate planning process. The goal is not to provide you with a book or comprehensive analysis of financial planning generally. So use these discussions to build awareness, as a catalyst to engage in a dialogue with your wealth manager or financial planner, insurance consultant, and your CPA about these topics, and be sure that your financial planning and estate planning are coordinated. Without that, your goals won't be achieved.

## INVESTMENT STANDARDS

Many people living with COPD, especially if they have additional health challenges, may benefit from establishing a revocable living trust. See Chapter 12. Everyone living with COPD should have a power of attorney. A trustee under a trust, and an agent under a power of attorney, are fiduciaries. This means that they are in positions of trust and must conduct themselves accordingly. When a fiduciary handles investment decisions, he or she must be cognizant of the Prudent Investor Act, a law that governs how investments should be handled. While the laws vary by state, the Prudent Investor Act will generally require that investments be diversified, that the level of risk be appropriate for the goals set, and so on. Fiduciaries must also be mindful of the investment provisions of the governing document (e.g., the trust or power of attorney). What this all means to you is that when you plan your trust or power of attorney, consider how the provisions you write will affect your fiduciary's actions. If, for example, you have a closely held business that you want retained in your family, your documents should authorize, perhaps even direct, the fiduciaries to retain the business. If you wish to permit a religious or socially oriented investment strategy, if that strategy meets your religious or other personal beliefs, your documents must address this.

While you can personally choose to ignore the Prudent Investor Act when you invest your own money, caveat emptor! These laws are based on modern portfolio theory, which, through careful analysis of volumes of investment performance data, have demonstrated that you can reduce risk and maintain (or increase) return through rational diversification of your investments. Even if you're pretty astute as an investor, consider consulting with an independent investment adviser to get input as to your budget, financial plan, and investment strategy. And even if you're pretty independent minded, consider adhering to many of the requirements of the Prudent Investor Act, because they do make sense. Finally, given the health challenges that you must have if you're reading this book, having an independent financial adviser guide you (or even just periodically consult with you) is a great way to build a team of advisers around you, and a written track record of what you want done for the future in the event you will need that assistance.

## FINANCIAL PLANNING CONSIDERATIONS

Investment planning is an integral part of your estate and related planning. If your funds are not properly invested, your estate could be dissipated before you die rendering all your careful planning and tailored documents useless. Just as with many of the estate planning documents and techniques discussed above, many investment advisers and financial planners operate under misconceptions and apply incorrect generalizations about investment planning for those with chronic illness, and COPD is no exception. As mentioned earlier in this book, you need to be proactive and explain your health conditions to your advisers.

Your symptoms might make it difficult to manage assets today, but even if not, they may make it more difficult in the future as symptoms worsen. Also, don't forget the impact of your exercise, diet, and medical appointment regimen on the time you will have to devote to financial and investment matters. Be realistic. It's always better to seek help before you need to do so, than to need help and not seek it until after it is too late.

Consolidation and simplification of investments and other assets is strongly advisable. This approach will provide you with a greater ability to control resources even if physical or cognitive impairments make record keeping more difficult. Comprehensive financial planning should be undertaken to ensure that your resources will not run out. Such planning should consider and address:

❖     A reduction in work time and hence salary, or cessation of work altogether.

❖     Possible shortened career duration.

❖     Your receipt of money from an existing disability insurance policy (presumably purchased prior to your diagnosis).

❖     Near- and long-term effects on the earnings of a caregiver partner/ spouse.

❖     Costly medications, if insurance now or in the future may not cover them.

❖     Modifications to make to your home to accommodate your challenges.

In light of these and other factors, you should reevaluate your investment risk tolerance, return needs, and resulting investment allocation. With new uncertainties and costs, you may need to reduce the previous accepted level of investment risk. On the other hand, your budget projections might demonstrate that the new financial reality requires greater investment risks to meet new needs and goals. The key is to quantify what your budget and future needs, and financial resources appear to be. Stress test the results (i.e., evaluate the results under different scenarios such as better or worse market performance, high-end versus low-end estimates for certain critical expenses, etc.). None of this is an exact science, but doing the math homework will give you a dramatically better shot at meeting your goals than not addressing these issues.

These decisions could also have an impact on the investment provisions in your will and trusts. Prior to diagnosis, your documents may have included broad investment clauses permitting holding non-liquid, non-diversified assets, closely held business interests and so forth, all without regard to Prudent Investor Act limitations. These may now warrant revision to meet the mandates of the Prudent Investor Act, and may include risk-return analysis and maintaining a diversified portfolio that considers all relevant factors. In very simple terms, the Prudent Investor Act mandates that funds be invested in a diversified manner to reduce risk and maximize return.

## BUSTING INVESTING MYTHS

The knee-jerk reactions of some wealth managers and estate planners to clients with chronic illness can be dangerously wrong.

❖ **Myth:** Investors with chronic illness need liquidity.

❖ **Reality:** Some do, many don't. You may actually have significant savings, an insurance safety net, and continued earnings from employment. Others will not. Making assumptions that planning is "standard" won't serve you well. While some people living with chronic illness prefer more liquidity in their investment portfolios than others, for many investors with chronic illness the opposite may be a sounder approach. If substantial liquidity is appropriate for you, the remainder of your investments may take on what is sometimes called a barbell investment strategy. More weight will be given to more aggressive equities to offset the low returns anticipated on the overweight allocation to cash. Bear in mind that this strategy may have higher volatility risk than alternative strategies. For example, if you were diagnosed in your late 60s with COPD and have worked and saved prudently your entire life, your decision process may be quite different than someone who was diagnosed in their early 40s and has made only modest inroads in saving for retirement.

❖ **Myth:** Clients with chronic illness should invest with a short-term time horizon.

❖ **Reality:** Some should, many shouldn't. Many advisers mistakenly "lump" all chronic illnesses together and mistakenly presume a shortened life expectancy. Most people living with COPD will have a relatively normal life expectancy, unless another disease (comorbidity) changes the analysis. So a short time horizon could make any investment and financial planning decisions based on that mistaken assumption dangerously wrong. In contrast to most people with COPD, those people living with Alzheimer's disease generally survive for only about four to eight years after diagnosis, although some have survived much longer. Most people with COPD need long-term investment planning, not short term. Even for people with a shorter than average life expectancy, the magnitude of their wealth and the nature of their estate plan may create long-term investment horizons for certain "buckets" of assets that will almost assuredly be bequeathed to heirs or spent. But there is significant variation, not only between different illnesses, but even among people living with the same illness. Focus on the real facts that pertain to your situation and make certain your advisers do the same.

❖    **Myth:** Clients with chronic illness need special needs trusts.

❖    **Reality:** Some chronic illnesses strike young people. However, others strike late in life. Thus, many people living with chronic illness have had a full work/career life and may have significant assets. For these individuals, a special needs arrangement (e.g., in a spouse's will) may not be appropriate. So the real answer depends on the severity of your COPD, the magnitude of your wealth, state law that governs this planning, and other factors. You should consult with an attorney in your state who specializes in this type of planning, called an "elder law attorney," to ascertain what steps might be advisable. For example, the attorney might recommend that your spouse and anyone else leaving you assets bequeath them in a special needs trust (SNT) for your benefit rather than directly to you.

❖    **Myth:** Budget projections are standard.

❖    **Reality:** Some financial planners actually use the same canned investment and other assumptions for most of their clients, chronic illness or not. Others assume that all clients with chronic illness will live on government aid. Sometimes true, often not. Many people diagnosed with COPD, for example, may have already acquired long-term care coverage. On the other hand, if your health insurance changes its coverage for your drug therapies, for example, your entire financial picture could be affected if a previously modest monthly co-payment now triggers a substantial annual cost. What might the cost of modifying your home be? What about the cost of providing accommodations for a live-in caregiver? The "what-ifs" to budget properly are more complex and uncertain than for most people, and these issues need to be factored into the planning.

❖    **Myth:** If you face the uncertainties of a chronic illness, you cannot bear the same level of risk other investors would accept.

❖    **Reality:** Many chronically ill people have substantial wealth and can make the same risk/return decisions any other investor might choose.

Most people living with COPD will live for a normal life expectancy, which may be a decade or many decades. Structuring a portfolio with inadequate risk might leave you unprotected against the ravages of inflation, or worse, broke. In fact, some investors living with COPD may feel quite comfortable accepting a higher level of risk in order to meet long-term investment goals.

EXAMPLE

Jill Forsythe is 48 years old and living with COPD. Jill has had a successful career in management, but anticipates that she will have to cut back on her hours by age 55 because of fatigue and the hours she will have to devote to her care. A possible asset allocation for Jill might be heavily weighted toward equities and alternative investments to create sufficient wealth to retire at 55, an allocation that might strike the typical 48-year-old as somewhat aggressive. The disease may have given Jill sufficient financial maturity to realize that, if her work career has to extend another couple of years if the target is missed, the long-term plan would be challenging but still possible (e.g., working with further reduced hours, or out of a home-based office). The key point is that Jill, in consultation with her financial planner, has affirmatively decided to take on more investment risk after to her diagnosis, so that she can get closer to meeting her necessary retirement goals in spite of cutting back hours for what she believes will be the last 10 years of her career. If Jill does not tighten her budget and ramp up her investment risk, the lower savings she will realize when she cuts back at age 55 will hinder her ability to retire with the financial security she had hoped for.

## OTHER NUANCES OF WEALTH MANAGEMENT FOR THE CHRONICALLY ILL

Because you have a chronic illness, you need to view wealth management and estate planning differently from the way people without a chronic illness do. Some aspects of planning that your illness may have an effect on are discussed below:

❖ **Agent and Fiduciary.** Your COPD might cause your investment advisers to accept investment and other direction from a fiduciary acting on your behalf (e.g., the agent under your durable power of attorney). Set up a meeting early in the relationship with your planner so that you can be sure that your planner understands how your power of attorney, revocable trust, and other documents might affect your agents. Be certain that the decision-making authority and mechanisms your planner and other agents need to best serve you throughout your relationship are provided in the documents. Don't assume the documents will meet your needs. Have the adviser (or better yet, your adviser's attorney) review the provisions governing decision making, power and authority, investment allocation, and so on. Make certain that your adviser has a copy of your power of attorney and revocable living trust, if you have one.

❖ **Needs Analysis.** To properly budget and estimate future needs and services, consider having a consultation with your financial planner and a geriatric consultant or care manager. An independent evaluation and report can better clarify your current and potential future circumstances and needs, which will help guide your wealth manager, estate planner, and other advisers. For example, a care manager may be able to assess whether or not you might need home modifications, the types of modifications you might need, and estimates of their costs. These and other refinements can be incredibly helpful in making a rather generic budget and financial plan more specific to your situation. Even small differences in incremental costs of dealing with COPD, if compounded over decades of your remaining lifetime, can result in significant errors if ignored.

❖ **Estate Planning Techniques.** Your investment planning must be coordinated with your estate planning. Don't let your adviser assume that you need not engage in estate tax minimization if in fact you have sufficient assets to warrant such planning. You must also inform your adviser how planning can proceed, but with a bias toward addressing your personal goals, such as retaining control over assets, and investment assets in particular, in light of the health uncertainties you face.

❖ **Annual Meetings.** Annual meetings are strongly recommended. Circumstances can change. Feelings will change. If you were recently diagnosed, it will take some time for you to come to terms with your illness and prognosis. As you gain a greater understanding of your condition, estate planning and personal and investment decisions will all evolve. Remember, estate planning meeting is not only about updating a will, it's about the ancillary planning discussed throughout this book, coordinating advisers, building a relationship so your advisers will have more personal knowledge of your objectives should an emergency arise, and addressing the inevitable loose ends that every plan has.

## QUESTIONS TO DISCUSS WITH YOUR FINANCIAL PLANNER

Financial planning is quite unique for each individual; many of the really important questions you need to address will come to light while you're meeting with your planner, so be sure to take notes and assemble an action list for later follow-up. Some of the questions you might want to consider discussing include the following:

❖     How can I estimate possible large future expenses that should be reserved for? Do you have any insight into these? Is it advisable to have a care plan prepared for additional input? If so, how often should it be updated?

❖     How can I analyze economically the net benefit of continuing to work? How long must I work to secure my financial future? How can I estimate the effect my illness will have on my earnings?

❖     Can you make the accommodations that I need for meetings to make it easier for me?

❖     How will my financial plan affect my estate and insurance planning?

❖     How frequently should we schedule review meetings?

❖     How can you help me determine the amount of risk I should, or must, tolerate in my investment plan in order to achieve my financial goals?

❖     How can we determine the minimum cash or liquidity that I need so that I can feel secure?

❖     What if there is another stock market meltdown like 2008–2009?

❖     How can I ensure adequate cash flow over the long term?

❖     What can be done to simplify and automate as many financial tasks as possible?

❖     How can we involve my CPA so that he or she can provide some measure of oversight to the financial and investment planning you are recommending without adding unduly to my costs?

## QUESTIONS TO DISCUSS WITH YOUR INSURANCE PLANNER

Insurance is an integral part of every financial plan. Elsewhere in the book is a list of some of the types of coverage to consider (property, casualty and liability, etc.). Don't assume that simply because you've been diagnosed with COPD there is no insurance planning relevant to your situation. There is. What types of coverage and what you should do will all depend on your circumstances, but don't dismiss insurance planning without first evaluating options with an expert. There is a host of questions you should discuss with your financial planner. These will vary depending on your financial position, health, and so forth. Here are some suggestions:

❖     Are the types and limits of insurance coverage I have sufficient? Are the companies I am insured with fiscally secure? Is there anything I should change? One cost savings measure might be to increase deductibles. If I'm cutting back on work or other activities because of health issues (or even just changes in desires) can coverage be changed or modified?

❖     If there are gaps in my insurance coverage, what if anything can be done? Do have a personal excess liability policy that is coordinated with my underlying homeowners and automobile coverage?

❖     How will my financial plan affect my estate and insurance planning?

❖     How frequently should we schedule review meetings?

❖     How can you help me determine the amount of deductibles I should, or must, tolerate in my insurance policies in order to achieve my financial goals?

❖     What benefits does my existing disability policy provide and who should analyze it?

❖     What benefits does my existing long-term care policy provide and who should analyze it?

❖     What benefits might my caretaker spouse/partner obtain from his or her existing long-term policy? Should coverage be obtained if he or she doesn't have it?

❖     What role does my existing life insurance play in my planning? Are there options under my existing policies that should be acted upon? What should I do with existing life insurance coverage? Sell it? Continue it? Convert it?

# CHAPTER SUMMARY

This chapter has provided an overview of the financial, insurance, and related planning that should form the foundation for your estate, disability, and retirement planning. This chapter should be viewed as at most a cursory mention of this vital topic, but it has been included to make certain that you don't overlook proper planning and integration of your financial and insurance planning with your estate planning. Importantly, since every aspect of planning changes when you are living with COPD, many of the steps you should consider have been explained in a manner that applies to you.

## CHAPTER 6

# POWER OF ATTORNEY

## AUTHORIZING SOMEONE TO TAKE LEGAL ACTION FOR YOU

## INTRODUCTION

IF YOU ARE SICK OR DISABLED, who can handle financial, legal, and tax matters for you? Who can pay your bills so your bank doesn't foreclose on your mortgage, or the utility company doesn't cut off your phone, heat, and power? And who will take care of other emergencies that you are not able to handle?

If you are married, you cannot automatically count on your spouse to have the legal authority to handle every emergency just because of the marital relationship. Don't assume that your spouse has legal authority to sign your name. He or she does not. If you have a joint checking account, your spouse can sign checks from that account because it is joint, not by virtue of being your spouse. That's not much to rely upon in an emergency.

The best answer to the questions posed above is a legal answer: a document called a "power of attorney." A power of attorney is the most important and one of the most common estate planning documents. It is a contract in which you (called the "grantor") delegate ("grant") to another person (called your "attorney in fact" or "agent") the power and right to act on your behalf in the event you are ill, injured, unavailable, or unable to act on your own behalf for any reason. Your agent is given the important responsibility of handling your financial, legal, and tax matters in the event of any emergency, which prevents you from taking the necessary actions.

The power of attorney is one of the most important documents to consider during estate planning. But it is also one of the most frequently overlooked, and one of the most misunderstood. The power of attorney can be a very simple document, perhaps a one-page form purchased at a local stationery store. (But see the discussion below on the risk of using this kind of form.) A power of attorney can also be a far more complex and lengthy document prepared by an attorney to deal with a specific business transaction.

Important rules concerning power of attorney documents differ from state to state (e.g., what formalities are required to sign the power). Be certain to consult with an attorney in your state as to the specific rules that apply to you. For example, some states limit to certain close relatives the people you may name to act for you. In some states it may be advisable to file (record) your power of attorney in the appropriate governmental office, such as a county clerk. That will make it a public document so that anyone who has to rely upon it can find it in the public records. Some states don't permit what is called a "springing power." This is explained below.

While it is important that everyone over age 18 have a power of attorney, appointing an agent after being diagnosed with COPD is even more important. Depending on your prognosis, you are likely to have a substantially greater need than the average person of your age to have someone step in to help you. Depending on the current status and anticipated progression of your illness, this may even be a certainty. As with all of your estate planning documents, the impact of your diagnosis should result in modifications to the typical planning and perhaps even the form. You should consider providing detailed instructions to your agent. A personal meeting to explain the role as agent, provide an overview of the types of actions that might be necessary (e.g., pay certain bills), some financial data (no need to divulge all), is advisable. This should be followed up with a letter the agent can refer back to when he or she operates.

When planning how you should handle a power of attorney, consider: How likely is it that you may suffer any cognitive impairment from your disease? How should that be addressed? The possible courses of your disease (not just the most likely course) may lead you to consider the limits or allowances on the powers you give your agent under your power of attorney.

## TERMINOLOGY USED IN POWERS OF ATTORNEY

Lawyers, like all specialists, love jargon. It's not that they're conspiring to make matters complicated—it's because the use of specific technical terms permits precision. Understanding some of the jargon used for powers of attorney will make it easier to work with your lawyer and plan and create the document you need.

## POWER OF ATTORNEY

"Power of attorney" refers to the document in which you name a trusted person to be your agent and carry out your wishes.

## DURABLE POWER OF ATTORNEY

The document is called a "durable" power of attorney because it gives your agent the right to act even in the event of your disability. If your power of attorney is not durable, it would become invalid upon your becoming disabled. That's not of much use, so the document should include a statement to the effect that: "This power of attorney will remain in force and effect even if I'm disabled." In most states, this is all that's necessary to achieve this important goal; however, requirements of applicable state law should be complied with in all cases. Check with a local attorney.

## GENERAL POWER OF ATTORNEY

A general power enables your agent to take care of any matter that the power of attorney form or state law permits. This usually includes a very long and broad list of legal, financial, and other matters. In many, but not all, situations, you would want to grant the person you designate a general power of attorney. The rationale for this is simple. When you're signing the power of attorney document in most cases you cannot have any idea what specific tasks the agent may have to perform to help you out years in the future. The broader the powers granted, the more likely the actions you require will be covered. But the flip side to that coin is that the broader the powers, the more potential for an unscrupulous agent to take advantage of you. The sample form illustrated in the appendix to this chapter is a general power of attorney. There are, however, some situations in which such a broad grant of power is not necessary, and sometimes perhaps not even appropriate.

## SPECIAL POWER OF ATTORNEY

A special power is a power that is limited in scope. It allows your agent to handle only one particular transaction or perhaps one type of transaction. A special power might prove too limiting, even useless, for general planning if you become disabled because you don't know what legal and financial issues you're going to face and what problems will arise. Because you cannot possibly know what type of limited powers should be given to an agent under a special power of attorney, your best option for general protection and estate planning is to give someone a general power that will be broadly effective so if you're unable to manage your affairs, your agent will be empowered to handle any foreseeable financial matters. So why would you ever want a special or limited power? The examples below provide typical scenarios in which this type of power might apply.

### EXAMPLE

Assume you're going out of town for a business meeting that cannot be canceled. Unfortunately, your contract for selling your house is scheduled to close that same week, and you have to be present at the closing to sign papers. What do you do? A special power of attorney could be an option. You could name a trusted friend or family member as your agent to sign any documents necessary to complete your house closing. This is a special power because you've only given the agent one limited right. After the house closing is completed, the agent's authority ends.

### EXAMPLE

Assume you're selling your contracting business because symptoms related to your COPD have worsened and you find the physical labor too difficult. While you do pretty well on most days, some days are very tough, and you've had a couple of flare-ups. Not knowing how you will feel on the day of the closing, and worrying that the stress of selling the business you've operated for decades may itself trigger a flare-up, since the date has to be agreed upon well in advance, you have your lawyer who is handling the closing prepare a special durable power of attorney authorizing your agent to sign all the documents relating to the sale of the business "just in case." This is a special power because you've only given the agent one limited right, which is limited even further because the agent is authorized to act on your behalf only if you are too ill to do so yourself. After the sale of your business is completed, the agent's authority ends.

### KEY

This is yet another example of why it is so important to ensure that your attorney and other advisors understand your illness and how it affects you.

## BUSINESS POWER

If you own or operate a business and are temporarily hospitalized or become incapacitated, who will sign checks, and address business or professional practice matters? Who will sign the payroll and other checks and ensure that your employees continue running the business if you are out? Improper planning can cause undue delay and hardship during an already difficult time, and this could be a significant problem. Properly prepared durable powers of attorney are an important part of the solution if your business or practice is organized as a "sole proprietorship." A sole proprietorship is simply a business you own personally, i.e., without an entity. This contrasts to a business that is organized in a legal form (corporation, limited liability company, partnership, etc.). A "special" power granted to a business adviser or colleague (or in the case of a professional practice, a similarly licensed professional) can be an essential aspect of protection.

Under certain circumstances, you may need to combine several documents. For example, you may wish to grant a limited power of attorney to a close colleague to authorize him or her to perform certain functions relating to your medical practice during a period when you are ill or otherwise unavailable. Such a power of attorney may even provide for compensation. You may execute another power of attorney granting your spouse the right to handle all personal financial matters.

If your business is organized as a corporation, you may need to sign minutes or a unanimous written consent for the corporation naming the intended person as an officer of the corporation (e.g., vice president) in order to vest in this individual the powers needed to act on behalf of the corporation.

If your business is owned as a limited liability company you could have your lawyer structure the business as a manager managed limited liability company. That means a person is designated as the manager, who does not have to be an owner ("member"). You could be the initial sole manager and sole member. But the legal document that governs the business, called an "operating agreement," can designate a person to serve as manager if you cannot (called "successor manager"). This will provide within the structure of the business entity a form of disability management succession that your power of attorney provides for personal succession in the event of a flare-up, long-term hospitalization, or worsening cognitive issues.

The right approach is to consult your business attorney (often called "corporate" attorney) and make sure that you have appropriate precautions in place.

## SPRINGING POWER OF ATTORNEY

COPD creates a number of circumstances in which a springing power of attorney might be applicable. This power is one that only springs into use (i.e., your agent's power becomes effective) when you become disabled. This prevents your agent from having any authority until you are actually disabled and need assistance. While this may be the best approach if you prefer not to grant any authority to your agent until it becomes absolutely necessary, it is not a simple conclusion. As noted above, some states won't respect a springing power. So depending on where you live, the springing power may not be an option. The strongest argument against the springing power of attorney is that you should not grant any power of attorney unless you trust the person named. If trust is not an issue, why restrict the power of attorney until you become disabled? This could raise questions as to when, or even whether, the power of attorney has become effective (i.e., whether you are disabled and when you actually became disabled).

Springing powers can get more sophisticated. You could have a primary (first named) agent's power effective immediately upon signing your power of attorney (e.g., your spouse or partner), while the authority of alternate agents (children, friends) becomes effective only when those agents can legally demonstrate your disability. If you feel comfortable naming certain people as agent if their power is effective only if you are disabled, consult an estate planning attorney in your state.

The typical advice for someone with a chronic illness is not to use a springing power of attorney, but rather to sign a power that is effective immediately. The rationale for this view is that you may be putting your agent (as well as yourself) in a precarious position because you are implicitly burdening that agent with the very real possibility that he or she will have to prove that you are disabled.

The problems of triggering a springing power are common to all people, not just those with chronic illness, but there are situations where it might be warranted and workable. Depending on the nature of your illness, the power may only have to be triggered once, when your level of incapacity reaches a point where an agent has to permanently take over. So if you have severe COPD and realistically believe that a level of cognitive impairment that will hinder your managing your financial affairs is likely, a springing power of attorney may not be unreasonable in that it will likely only have to be "sprung" once. Although your attorney may still maintain that a power of attorney that is effective upon signing is preferable, if you feel strongly about deferring the time until someone can act on your behalf, you can use a springing power of attorney.

More significantly, if your COPD is punctuated by flare-ups between which you can remain in control of your affairs, but during which you might need help, this generic advice is not particularly useful. For most people with COPD, the springing power option may not really provide any significant benefit, and it will introduce a level of complexity and confusion. If you have a springing power, any flare-up will raise issues as to the status of that power and will have to be addressed.

KEY

> You don't need to hire a specialist in estate planning for chronic illness or a financial planner that focuses on clients with chronic illness. Too often such advertised "specialties" are just a marketing gimmick. You want to hire competent professionals whom you can apprise in detail of your situation. A good estate planning attorney will quickly understand the nuances this book raises and will help tailor them to you to the extent deemed appropriate in his or her professional judgment.

## IS YOUR CHRONIC ILLNESS PUNCTUATED BY SPORADIC FLARE-UPS?

Your COPD may follow an on-again, off-again pattern (i.e., intermittent flare-ups that are associated with particularly hot, humid days with a high smog index). What this means is that you experience periods of relapse (when your symptoms increase in severity) and periods of recovery when you will hopefully regain any cognitive function temporarily lost, or overcome any confusion the flare-up triggered, or recover physically and this may call for special planning alternatives.

If you have a flare-up or attack, you may want your agent to assume control as soon as you are unable to do so. However, if the likely time frame for the duration of a flare-up is relatively short, and you've heeded the financial and organizational advice in preceding chapters, you may not have a pressing need for an agent to step in. So while you should still plan, the point is that other planning steps you take lessen the urgency of having an agent to act, and significantly reduce the responsibilities and time an agent will need to act if required.

You assuredly want control to revert to you as soon as you become able once more to handle your affairs. Springing powers are not designed to match these needs because your agent would periodically have to go through the process of demonstrating your disability and then recovery, thus hindering quick action to help you in the event of a flare-up and also potentially hindering your right to resume acting on your own behalf. In a worst-case scenario, implementing a springing power may mean that by the time your agent has legally demonstrated his or her ability to serve, you may have already been released from the hospital, or you may have regained whatever function temporary lost during a flare-up, and again be able to handle your own affairs.

### EXAMPLE • *Power of Attorney and COPD*

Jane Smith has COPD. She generally is fully capable of handling all financial, legal, and other matters that a durable power may cover. However, the impact of COPD has made it quite difficult to do many physical errands. Jane has remained on top of all her financial, business, and other affairs. In fact, she continues to operate a lucrative design business, only she now does so out of a home office to limit the physical demands required, and to make it easier to rest when she is fatigued. However, Jane's periods of activity are occasionally interrupted by periods when it is difficult or impossible for her cope without a assistance. These periods are unpredictable. If the appointment of the agent is effective immediately upon execution, unencumbered by the springing mechanism, the agent will be able to help during any such period without jumping through legal hoops. The agent can cede control back to Jane as soon as feasible, that is, as soon as the illness-related challenges have subsided. With a springing power, by the time the agent can legally demonstrate Jane's disability, the relapse will probably have subsided. Jane would probably, however, be better served by organizing her design business as a limited liability company, having the corporate attorney who sets up the entity create a successor manager in the operating agreement as explained above, and limiting her agent under her durable power to personal non-business matters.

Another issue Jane faces is that, although she is fully competent to handle all her affairs, her mobility issues and fatigue often make it a chore to physically go to the bank. Although Jane has automated as many banking tasks as possible online, business issues demand her presence at the bank at least several times a week. Signing the typically proposed immediate (not springing) broad and general (covers everything) power of attorney would cause Jane to cede more control than she really wants to give an agent. This dilemma and similar circumstances can be addressed by her signing a limited bank power of attorney to permit a designated person to handle matters pertaining to only her business bank account. The hybrid approach discussed in the next section might also provide a different method that might appeal to Jane.

## HYBRID APPROACH BEST FOR SOME CHRONIC ILLNESSES

Another possible answer to Jane's dilemma provides a creative and flexible approach that will benefit many people with chronic illness. It is an approach that maximizes the benefits of springing durable powers of attorney for those facing sporadic flare-ups. It is important to note that such hybridization must be approached carefully and only with the assistance of a professional well versed in the associated legal considerations.

If you have a chronic illness but also have long periods when you are capable of handling all of your financial legal and tax matters, you don't want to lose control over your affairs during those periods. These periods may be interrupted by brief periods of hospitalization or flare-up when it is difficult or impossible to cope without an agent's assistance. In most situations your agent will not have to make the major long-term decisions that an agent for someone suffering with, by comparison, Alzheimer's disease dementia, may have to make. Major decisions can probably be deferred until you recover from a flare-up. This obviously does not apply to individuals with significant and permanent cognitive decline from severe COPD or some other significant health condition ("comorbidity").

This makes the generic springing mechanism a cumbersome tool that often creates more problems than it solves. An alternative is to consider using two separate powers of attorney to protect you while simultaneously preserving your independence.

The first document is a typical general durable power of attorney with springing provisions for agents. Should your disability increase to the degree an agent will have to operate on an ongoing basis, this broad power of attorney, similar to that used by many estate planners (in states where it is permissible), will be available. It includes a springing mechanism, with appropriate modifications that are tailored to address your challenges of COPD that will trigger it. The sample clause below illustrates how this power can be tailored.

## Sample Clause

"The Grantor shall be deemed disabled when Grantor is unable to manage Grantor's affairs and property effectively for a period anticipated being more than thirty (30) days [This duration was included to avoid triggering the power of any successor agent to act, as a result of a short-term hospitalization or flare-up.] Disability may be determined to exist for reasons such as mental illness, mental deficiency, physical illness or disability, advanced age, chronic use of drugs, chronic intoxication, or for any other reason allowable by law. In addition to any other method allowed by law to determine disability, it shall be deemed conclusive proof that the Grant to the Alternate Agent is effective upon a sworn statement being executed by both Grantor's attending pulmonologist and psychiatrist."

The second document is a limited power of attorney, effective immediately with no springing provision. This power limits the agent's rights to those matters that might need addressing during a short-term flare-up or hospitalization. In this type of limited document you don't necessarily need to authorize your agent to make gifts, change beneficiary designations on insurance and retirement plans, sell real estate (like your home), and so on. Those major decisions probably can wait until you recover from the short-term flare-up, or are released from the hospital. This provides a secure option in the event the agent under a broad springing power is unable to help you (i.e., because of the difficulty and time required to demonstrate your disability). This approach does not cede powers that you might prefer to retain over your affairs for the foreseeable future, and that your illness may never impact, yet it should facilitate quick assistance if needed. The purported protection some people believe a springing power provides (i.e., by limiting your agent's right to act until you are proven disabled) are unnecessary in this power of attorney because of the limitations on the authority you give the agent in the document. The same people could be named agents in both the springing general power of attorney discussed above, and this immediate limited power, to avoid any conflict between the agents appointed under each document.

## COMMON ISSUES AFFECTING POWERS OF ATTORNEY

### DIFFERENT TYPES OF POWERS YOU MIGHT SIGN

There are many different types of powers of attorney that should be considered. In most instances more than one type of power will be worth considering for optimal flexibility and protection. Care must be exercised, however, because each type of power presents its own unique risks and shortcomings. You also want consistency among all forms.

### *Bank/Brokerage Firm Standard Form*

The first and simplest power of attorney is to call your bank, mutual fund, and the brokerage houses where you have your primary accounts, and ask for their standard forms. These may be as simple as a 3 × 5 card on which you fill in the account name, account number, and the name of the person you want to be your agent. You will sign it at the bank or in front of a notary. This might be an excellent step to take. If the bank has a power of attorney on file, it is most likely to readily accept that agent's signature without question. Just be certain that you implicitly trust the person you are naming in this capacity. These forms tend to be simple, no "springing" powers, no authority to address non-banking matters, but perhaps no limit on banking steps that can be taken as to your accounts. Be careful to ascertain whether the form power applies to only one account, or every account at that institution. For example, if you have a large home equity line of credit at that bank, will the bank form power you sign to authorize your agent to handle routine bill paying also permit the agent to access this large line or credit?

### *Standard/Statutory State Preprinted Form*

Another type of power of attorney is the "standard" form used in your state. Most states have one or perhaps two companies that print forms that lawyers, banks, and other financial institutions most commonly use in that state. These forms are often based on a state statutory power of attorney (provisions contained in a state law or "statute") and, as such, should track the language of that state statute. Obtaining access to one of those forms (commonly, they can be purchased for a few dollars in an office supply store or legal supply house or are available online) can enable you to put in place a simple, basic level of protection. The powers of attorney in almost all instances must be notarized and, in many instances, someone should witness your signature as well.

These forms are typically one to six pages, some are relatively simple, widely accepted and recognized by all institutions, attorneys, etc., in the state. Unfortunately, some of the standard state forms are unbelievably complicated, and contain a significant number of optional provisions, exhibits, and other nuances. While one advantage that some of these forms have is that they are short, simple, inexpensive, and readily accepted, unfortunately not all are. The complex ones can be so daunting that you need an attorney to guide you through the maze. An important caution—you should be certain to review the provisions of these forms with an attorney.

## Comprehensive Power

Perhaps the most important type of power of attorney, for some people, is an attorney-drafted comprehensive durable power of attorney tailored specifically for their circumstances. This could be important because the standard forms lack many important provisions. Before retaining an attorney, make sure he or she is a specialist in the estate planning area. You should inquire whether the attorney understands the provisions that are included in a more comprehensive custom power of attorney that the standard form might lack. These special provisions could include the "right" to make gifts, the right to deal with the Internal Revenue Service ("IRS"), and more comprehensive lists of rights or authority granted to the agent. The right to make gifts is essential. Without specifically providing for the agent's right to make a gift, the IRS (under the laws of many states) will not accept the agent's gifts as binding for tax purposes. This can be very important because starting and continuing an aggressive gift program is an essential estate and asset protection planning tool. The ability to continue this plan or program in the event of your disability could be essential to saving significant state or federal (depending on the future changes in the law) estate tax dollars for your heirs. Specific and detailed authority to deal with the IRS is important. In the event of an IRS lien, whether mistakenly or appropriately placed on one of your accounts, it is essential that authority be given to the agent to deal with the IRS. Standard forms may not include such language, and that could create difficulties in the event of your significant or permanent disability. These are discussed in greater length later in this chapter.

Most comprehensive power of attorney forms are lengthy and contain broad detailed powers that grant the agent specific authority to deal with various types of situations. These include funding a revocable living trust to manage assets or minimize (even avoid) probate, dealing with business matters, and other matters that the standard forms or your state's law may not address.

## HOW MUCH AUTHORITY SHOULD AN AGENT BE GIVEN?

Deciding how much authority (and when) you should give your agent was discussed earlier in this chapter in the context of springing powers and crafting powers to fit your particular experience with COPD and any other health challenges. But this issue has broad implications beyond just the modifications discussed above that you might consider in light of your diagnosis. Powers of attorney are serious documents and can convey substantial authority. In the extreme, a power of attorney could enable the designated agent to change the entire dispositive scheme of your estate plan and gift away all assets. If you, as the grantor creating the power of attorney document, do not sufficiently trust someone to act in your best interest, other options should be considered, or the powers granted curtailed.

### EXAMPLE

An elderly widow was struggling with the challenges of severe COPD. Her nearest living relative was a nephew she saw a few times a year around the holidays. She named the nephew as agent under her general power of attorney. The nephew, realizing that his elderly aunt had limited mobility and limited awareness, began to actively use her funds for his own benefit. By the time he was discovered and the powers were revoked, he had nearly wiped out his aunt's estate. By then his aunt was too elderly and infirm to pursue the matter and had insufficient funds to hire an attorney. The nephew was never taken to task for his actions.

KEY

> If there is no one who is 100 percent trustworthy and you can afford it, consider setting up a revocable living trust with a bank or trust company as the sole trustee, co-trustee (perhaps with you), or as a successor co-trustee (along with a named family member or loved one). This can provide you (as the grantor setting up the trust) control over your assets and, when the institution is serving, provide independent oversight, for professional management of your investments. Liability insurance, government regulations and audits, and internal controls, which all large institutions have, provide greater assurance that your assets will be safe (see Chapter 12).

## POWER TO MAKE GIFTS

### POWER OF AGENT TO MAKE GIFTS GENERALLY

If you are unable to sign and distribute checks or meet with a lawyer to plan more complex gifts (e.g., the transfer of part of the ownership of a family business), a power of attorney can authorize your agent to make gifts to people you designate and take other actions to minimize your estate tax. You can authorize your agent, as many form powers do, to make annual gifts up to the maximum amount permitted without any gift tax consequences. This can be quite a large amount. It includes $13,000 gifts in any year to as many different people as you want. If you have a score of nieces and nephews, that's big bucks. The $13,000 amount is the allowable figure for 2012, but because it is indexed for inflation, a larger limit may apply in later years. In addition, you can also give unlimited amounts for tuition and medical payments (i.e., these payments are not counted toward the $13,000 annual exclusion figure). If that same score of nieces and nephews are all in private colleges, you could theoretically gift millions over a short time. The power of your agent to make gifts can be a tremendous planning tool, but it can add up to significant sums and be a risky source of abuse. The more dependent you are physically and emotionally on others as your COPD progresses, the greater risk you face that an agent, or someone else, might abuse these powers.

### EXAMPLE

A father began a regular gift program in which he and his wife join in making annual gifts of stock to each of their four children, their children's spouses, and their ten grandchildren. The gifts are each $24,000 in value, the maximum amount that can be given away in 2008 without any gift tax being due, for a total of $432,000 [(4 + 4 + 10) × $12,000 × 2] based on the 2008 maximum gift limit of $12,000 per donee. The father falls ill in December and is unable to sign the necessary documents to make a transfer for the year so the couple makes no gifts in that year. The couple could incur an unnecessary additional estate tax cost of as much as $216,000 (assuming a 50 percent maximum rate, although the actual federal rate is lower in 2012 and at the time of this writing the law in 2013 provides for a 55% rate and $1 million exemption, but it is uncertain what will actually occur) because this gift was not made. Had the father prepared an appropriate power of attorney, his agent may have been able to handle the paperwork necessary to make the gifts and eliminate this unnecessary estate tax burden. The figure would be higher if gifts for tuition and medical expenses were also made. Even if you're not subject to federal estate tax, your heirs might still face a costly state estate tax that, depending on state law, might be reduced by the gift planning. Even apart from gift planning, these provisions can provide critical help to an heir of yours who is having financial challenges.

## SHOULD YOU CURTAIL OR ELIMINATE GIFT POWERS IN LIGHT OF YOUR ILLNESS?

Most powers of attorney authorize agents to make gifts. The fatigue, possible cognitive impairment, or other symptoms of COPD may make it difficult for you to work at the same pace as previously. You may even have to cease working altogether. However, if employer-provided insurance coverage is lost, the out-of-pocket costs of treatment therapies could be tremendous. Thus, the economic reality of your diagnosis may warrant your reconsideration of gift powers. Although a broad gift authority may have been appropriate before your diagnosis, it might be advisable (following a diagnosis of a chronic illness) to expressly prohibit gifts in order to preserve resources for your own uncertain future. Also, if gifts really should not be necessary for Medicaid planning (see below), helping heirs, or saving taxes, it might just be wiser to expressly prohibit gifts to perhaps minimize that one avenue of potential financial abuse by an agent.

## POWER TO MAKE GIFTS FOR MEDICAID PLANNING

For many people with a chronic illness, the opposite approach to gifts may be preferable. The only way to ascertain this is to consult with an elder law attorney in your state (state laws differ significantly). Gifts to reduce assets for Medicaid purposes, for example, are becoming more prevalent. Making a transfer to reduce your assets requires that the power of attorney document include a broad gift power sufficient to give away all assets. If the clause is not sufficiently precise, governmental authorities will not respect the gifts. Such a power is so broad that it makes your power of attorney tantamount to a will in that it could become your primary dispositive document.

This raises a host of risks and issues. One issue is that most state laws have only a few requirements for a power of attorney to be effective (perhaps a notary and witnesses, etc.) compared to a will. When a power becomes your primary dispositive document, more care should be taken to ensure that certain safeguards exist. Think of how dangerous this could be without such safeguards. What if a home health worker has you sign a power of attorney form naming the aide as your agent while you're in a panic mode resulting from breathing difficulties and hence you are not really cognizant of the impact or consequences of what you are doing? Planning in advance, perhaps funding a revocable trust with an institutional trustee, can minimize the risk of this (if most of your assets are in the trust the home health aide as agent cannot affect them), and prevent much harm to your personal financial position. However, you need sufficient wealth for this to be feasible.

## SPECIAL CONSIDERATIONS FOR NAMING AGENTS

Because COPD could result in depression, anxiety, and unpredictable flare-ups, you should have to consider the availability and reliability of the agent you choose to name. Are they local? Can they arrange their schedule to be available in an emergency? Will they be able to become available quickly? If your COPD progresses to the degree of affecting your cognitive abilities, will your agent have time to serve for an extended period of time? You may also want to consider exactly whom you are appointing to this position. You may have previously assumed it would be one person, but does your diagnosis change that? When you told your family and friends about your illness, how did they react? Were they supportive? Understanding? Did they fully comprehend the impact of your disease? These are only a few of the nuances you might consider when choosing a person who will serve on your behalf. It may be difficult not to choose someone who expects to be chosen, but you must select the agent who best understands the impact of your disease, and who will best implement your wishes if you cannot, not the person who wants the appointment for ego or other reasons.

You should name several alternate agents as a precaution in the event that the primary agent is unable or unwilling to take the necessary actions. This is especially important since COPD won't necessarily reduce life expectancy but could result in your needing assistance for decades.

## OTHER PROVISIONS TO CONSIDER

### SHOULD YOUR AGENT BE GIVEN UNLIMITED POWER?

Your agent is generally authorized under most power of attorney documents to sign checks to pay for your medical care if you are hospitalized unexpectedly, handle your financial affairs generally, collect dividend checks, sell stocks and bonds, and carry out other legal, tax, and financial transactions. You may, however, wish to place restrictions on the scope of your agent's actions. This was discussed above in the context of how you might tailor your power of attorney to address the challenges of flare-ups and in light of a springing power. Remember, in all instances, the documents you sign must accomplish your goals and deal with your unique circumstances.

For example, you might limit your agent to permit only the payment of certain emergency expenses. You could expressly permit, or deny, your agent the right to sell your home or other real estate assets. Gift giving always warrants careful attention. The form provided in this book does not place any restrictions on your agent. If you are concerned, there are several options you should evaluate. Suppose, at some point, you realize that you may have selected the wrong person as agent. If you do not feel enough trust and confidence in this person, you may be motivated to restrict his or her powers or consider naming a different person as agent. In some cases, although it is cumbersome from an administrative perspective, and your attorney might even advise against it, you might have to appoint two co-agents to act together. The requirement for two signatures to approve any action may give you the assurance you want of neither agent violating your wishes or taking advantage of you. If you don't have anyone else to name, you might, as noted above, need a revocable living trust with an institution as trustee or as co-trustee (see Chapter 10).

## BUSINESS POWERS

The general discussion of business powers of attorney presented previously can also be reviewed for the purpose of setting limits, making modifications, or consideration of special nuances. If you have a business, such as a home-based business, which is not a corporation, partnership, or other entity, your agent under your power of attorney can be authorized to handle business matters for you. If your business is a corporation, partnership, limited liability company, or other type of entity, your power of attorney may not authorize you to take action for that entity. The entity itself must do that. If your business is a corporation, the shareholders should appoint people to serve as directors. The directors will generally appoint officers. Sometimes, but not always, all officers will be approved in the corporate minutes to sign bank accounts or handle other transactions. If you have these issues, don't take chances. In all such cases, consult with a corporate or business attorney and be certain that disability issues are addressed. A shareholder agreement and buy–sell agreement should be reviewed; if you don't have them, obtain them. If you operate a professional practice as a solo practitioner, you may be obligated to prepare a special limited power of attorney that provides a colleague or other licensed professional the right and obligation to manage your practice during an illness or disability and to transition your practice in the event of a permanent disability or death.

### EXAMPLE

Dana Jones is an attorney. She lives with her partner, Sarah, who is a clothing designer. Dana cannot name Sarah to handle legal matters for her law practice during a period of hospitalization or a flare-up when Dana cannot act. This is because Sarah is not licensed as an attorney and state law likely restricts who can act on behalf of a law practice. Dana therefore signs a limited ("special") durable (effective during disability) power of attorney to her colleague John Smith naming him as agent to manage her practice if she cannot do so. Dana gives Sarah a general (broad and all encompassing) durable power of attorney to handle all her personal financial matters. To avoid any conflict between Sarah and John, Dana provides in the general power to Sarah, one restriction—Sarah cannot make decisions concerning Dana's law practice. Furthermore, to better coordinate the activities of her two agents, Dana specifically authorizes Sarah to loan money to her law practice if necessary to help it through a period of time when she cannot work (e.g., to hire staff to cover for her).

## POWER TO DEAL WITH THE TAX AUTHORITIES

Dealing with the IRS can be an important matter. If you are unable to act, someone might need to sign a tax return for you (Form 1040 personal income tax return), or your home business (e.g., sales tax return), handle a tax audit, or address a lien placed on your accounts. This is an essential part of your planning. Your power of attorney might include some or all of the following (but check with your attorney):

❖  Specific rights to deal with the IRS (federal), state (state income tax, sales tax if you have a business), and local (e.g., town property tax) tax matters.

❖  Include your Social Security number in your power of attorney to facilitate your agent's work with tax authorities.

❖  Authorize your agent to sign any additional documents required for him or her to work with the various tax authorities, including but not limited to the IRS Form 2848 discussed below.

In addition to authorizing your agent to deal with the IRS and handle other tax matters in your power of authority, it can be helpful in certain circumstances to sign a special IRS form for this purpose. Always check with your accountant before doing this. Form 2848 is the IRS power of attorney that authorizes someone to act on your behalf with respect to tax matters. If you are audited by the IRS, one of the first things your attorney or accountant will request is that you sign a copy of Form 2848, "Power of Attorney and Declaration of Representative." This form must be on file with the IRS before any IRS agent will communicate with your accountant. Although the form is quite simple, there are a number of points and practical suggestions that can save time and reduce problems. It might be worthwhile to sign a number of extra copies of Form 2848 and have your accountant keep them in his or her file.

Read the form before you sign. You do not need to authorize your accountant to represent you for years and types of taxes other than what the particular audit is about. This is one way for you to control what your accountant is doing before seeking your approval. While this may be appropriate for most taxpayers, depending on your circumstances, a broader grant of authority may be preferable. There are boxes to check to tell the IRS where to send communication concerning the audit. Make sure both you and your accountant get copies. You don't want your accountant to indicate that correspondence should go only to him or her. You want copies sent to you (or your agent under your power of attorney), so you (or your agent) can monitor what is going on. Be careful with respect to the authorization to receive the payment of any refund. Only under a few special circumstances should you ever check the box authorizing your accountant to receive any refund check. Note that these boxes are sometimes checked by accountants without consultation with the taxpayer(s) signing the form. With this in mind, consider expressly directing any refunds to you or your agent.

## COMPENSATING YOUR AGENT

Generally, agents under a power of attorney are not compensated for their activities. However, you may want to consider whether your illness and the scope of activities your agent may be required to engage in on your behalf for a significant length of time warrants compensation. Should you compensate an agent who has to serve for a long time or at frequent intervals? If you do include a compensation clause, will you take into account when and how often your agent is likely to serve? You probably do not want to undercompensate an agent (even a family member) who serves full time for many months or years, as this may lead to less than full attention being paid to your financial issues. A common initial reaction is that a friend or family member doesn't need to get paid to help out. The reality is that your agent (at least those who take the job seriously) may have to handle paying your bills, filing your tax returns, managing your home repairs, and more for decades. That level of commitment should not go unpaid. If your agent becomes resentful of the time involved, or if the agent's spouse or partner becomes resentful of the commitment, compensation may alleviate some of the associated problems. Often, it is not even an issue of money. Your agent may be more comfortable financially than you are and may simply appreciate an acknowledgment of the efforts involved.

If you determine that compensation is warranted, compensation provisions should be tailored to the unique circumstances of your health challenges and other circumstances. The first question you must address is how to set the amount of compensation. Some attorneys use state law compensation for a trustee as a gauge for calculating an agent's compensation under a power of attorney. While that may work, it is a technical approach and legal advice will be necessary to interpret and implement such a provision. Moreover, while this type of compensation might make sense for someone with severe COPD compounded by other health issues (comorbidity), for whom the agent shoulders all responsibilities, this level of compensation might be excessive for you if your COPD is largely controlled and you generally can handle your affairs without assistance. Another way to address the issue is to evaluate how much help you might need and what might be a fair approach to compensating someone for that assistance. Perhaps the close family or friends you will name as your agents don't want compensation, and may not even need it. In that case, still consider paying compensation to that person. Most people assume "My brother [other family member] doesn't need to get paid." But if someone is paid they are not nearly as likely to grow resentful, and they'll most likely treat the tasks involved more seriously, not like "I'll get to it, I'm doing [your name] a favor."

For someone with COPD who has periodic hospitalizations or flare-ups during which assistance of an agent would be helpful, but thereafter regains the ability to manage his or her own aff airs, an agent's involvement may be sporadic and of short duration. Compensation based on statutory trustee fees, discussed above, would be impractical (prorating a statutory percentage of assets for a week long period) and may not be sufficient to cover the emergent and recurring nature of the agent's involvement. Thus, some stated minimum compensation each time the agent acts may be preferable. This type of compensation could change with changing circumstances. That is, if the agent begins to operate on a permanent basis, the compensation changes. So depending on your likely needs, a two-tier compensation structure might be advisable. Compensation under the limited special power of attorney discussed above could be provided as follows:

## *Sample Clause*

"In the event an agent acts hereunder, the agent shall be compensated at the rate of $X/week for any week in which the agent provides any services or acts hereunder, up to a maximum of Six (6) weeks in any given year. Compensation has been provided at a level to encourage the agent's involvement, and in recognition of the potential for having to act with little notice and at inconvenient times during a flare-up."

In plain English, this can be translated as "I want to reward and motivate the agents to act, even though he or she is a close friend or family member who would act without compensation." Even the occurrence of several acute events or hospitalizations during a year should readily be covered by the six-week period. But this cap will prevent the intended reward from becoming an unreasonable expense if a permanent issue arises. The second tier could be conpensation as a trustee discussed above.

## STATE-SPECIFIC ISSUES; RECORDING

As noted earlier in this chapter, it is important to address any particular issues of state law with your local attorney. In some states, particular attention should be paid to laws that limit whom you may name as an agent to certain close relatives. In other states it may be advisable to "file" the power of attorney document in the appropriate local court to make it "of record," as the example below illustrates.

### EXAMPLE

Dennis Frank has COPD and diabetes. As his diseases have progressed, he has stayed in control of all his legal and financial matters, but he now recognizes that he will need help. His only living family members, a son and aunt, are not appropriate to name as agents. His aunt is quite elderly, and his son, to Dennis' disappointment, has not been of much help. Dennis decides to name Jeff Green, his longtime CPA, as agent. In order to protect Jeff from a claim by Dennis' son, Dennis has an independent attorney prepare and supervise the signing of the power at a time when Jeff Green is not in the attorney's office. Denis also provided his attorney with a status letter from his pulmonologist dated only a few days before the appointment with the attorney confirming his health condition. Upon his attorney's recommendation, Dennis has the power of attorney recorded in the local county clerk's office. By making the appointment a matter of public record, Dennis has made it easier for Jeff to help him. The manner in which the power of attorney was recorded also makes it clear that Dennis was aware of the grant of the power to Jeff, and that Jeff was not in any manner hiding this appointment from Dennis' disenfranchised son.

## RELATIONSHIP OF POWER OF ATTORNEY RELATED TO OTHER ESTATE PLANNING DOCUMENTS

❖   *Revocable living trust.* A revocable living trust is not a substitute for a durable power of attorney. This is because a revocable living trust can only provide control to a trustee over the assets that have been transferred to the trust. A power of attorney, however, if broadly written, can give an agent access to all of your assets that have not been transferred to your living trust. Since a durable power of attorney immediately terminates on death, it can never be considered a substitute for a revocable living trust arrangement. But since you can never ensure all assets are transferred to a revocable living trust, you should always have a durable power of attorney document in your estate planning arsenal. For example, retirement plan accounts should generally not be transferred to a revocable living trust. Assets that may come to you in the future may not be transferred to the trust.

❖    *Will.* Since a durable power of attorney terminates on your death, it can never be considered a substitute for a will. Thus, a will is generally essential since it addresses the disposition of assets after your death, whereas the power of attorney will not. However, many powers give the agent broad enough authority to give away all assets, so the power of attorney begins to look like a will substitute, a situation that raises a range of concerns and issues.

❖    *Living will/health care proxy.* A financial/legal power of attorney should not be combined with a power of attorney for health care matters (a "health care proxy"). Many state laws, in fact, prohibit such combinations. Regardless of state law, the decisions are very different and often, the people named as agents in one document are different from those named as agents in the other document. Effort should be made to avoid authorizing your financial agent to make decisions concerning your health that would also affect health care issues over which a different agent has control. You don't want a conflict to develop where your financial agent refuses to pay for health care-related expenses and thereby seeks to control decisions you had intended to be within the purview of the person you named your health care agent. If you believe this type of conflict could occur, discuss it with your attorney and discuss possibly naming different agents or mandating that the financial agent shall be required to make payment for any health care decision made by your health care agent.

## Chapter Summary

A power of attorney, or several types of powers of attorney, could be the most important documents you sign to ensure that your financial, legal, tax, and certain other matters are properly addressed. If properly planned, powers can provide you with the maximum control over your affairs, while ensuring support and protection when you need it. These are serious documents that can involve your giving tremendous authority to the person(s) you appoint as your agent(s). They should not be treated as "standard" but should be carefully thought out and tailored to your needs.

**Caution:** The power of attorney document on the following pages is merely an illustration and you must discuss the appropriate form to use with an attorney in your state.

IMMEDIATE, GENERAL, AND DURABLE
# FINANCIAL POWER OF ATTORNEY

**KNOW ALL PERSONS BY THESE PRESENTS,** that I *CLIENTNAME (the "Grantor") (Social Security Number: *SOCIALSEC), residing at *CLIENT-ADDRESS, being of the age of majority under the laws of *STATENAME, and of sufficient capacity to conduct my business and financial affairs, in order to provide for management of Grantor's financial, legal and related, affairs in a more orderly fashion, hereby declare as follows:

1. **Appointment of Agent.** Grantor hereby makes, constitutes, and appoints ("Grant") *AGENT1-NAME residing at *AGENT-1ADDRESS, as Grantor's true and lawful Attorney-in-Fact and agent (the "Agent") for Grantor and in Grantor's name, place, and stead and for Grantor's benefit, or any alternate appointed in accordance with the provisions of this Power of Attorney (the "Agent").

2. **Alternate Agent.**
   a. If *AGENT1-NAME is unwilling or unable to act as Agent, Grantor appoints the first person able and willing to serve from the following list, as Grantor's Agent (the "Alternate Agent"):
   i. *AGENT2-NAME, who resides at *AGENT-2ADDRESS.
   ii. *AGENT3-NAME, who resides at *AGENT-3ADDRESS.
   iii. *AGENT4-NAME, who resides at *AGENT-4ADDRESS.
   b. Such person shall serve as Grantor's Agent. The timing of the appointment of the Alternate Agent shall be governed by the provision below, "Effective Date." Any rights or powers granted to the Agent are granted to the Alternate Agent, unless specifically provided to the contrary.

3. **Direction to Agent to Support Grantor and Named Persons.**
   a. The Agent is hereby authorized and directed to perform all acts reasonable and necessary to maintain Grantor's customary standard of living: to provide living quarters by purchase, lease, or other arrangement, or by payment of the operating costs of Grantor's existing living quarters, including interest, amortization payments, repairs, taxes, and so forth; to provide for the retention and payment of reasonably necessary domestic help for the maintenance and operation of Grantor's household; home health assistance and companion care if necessary; to finance or arrange for the purchase of other necessaries, including but not limited to clothing, transportation, entertainment, and incidentals; and to provide medical care, including the payment for experimental and novel medications and treatments if approved by Grantor's health care agent.
   b. The Agent is further authorized and directed to provide for the health, education, support, and maintenance of Grantor's spouse, and Grantor's children (whether or not such children are minors or dependents, and even if above the age of majority), in accordance with an ascertainable standard as defined in Code Section 2041 and the Regulations thereunder. Grantor recognizes that such transfers to or for the benefit of persons other than Grantor may constitute gifts and authorizes that such transfers be permitted and that such transfers not be restricted by the provisions below under the caption "Gifts." These support payments, however, shall not be in excess of those Grantor has traditionally paid, and shall give consideration to any worsening of Grantor's health status and the impact of that on Grantor's finances.
   c. Notwithstanding anything in this provision to the contrary, no Agent may exercise any power granted in this provision, or elsewhere in this Power of Attorney, in a manner that would cause any of Grantor's assets or estate to be taxable in the estate of any Agent. The foregoing sentence shall serve as an affirmative restriction and limitation on the right of any Agent acting hereunder.
   d. *Comment: Add provision and details concerning support of any pets.*

4. **Powers of Agent.** The Agent is hereby granted all the powers and rights necessary to effect Grantor's wishes, including, in addition to any power authorized by the laws of *STATENAME for an agent, the following:
   a. <u>General Financial Matters.</u>
   i. Request, ask, demand, sue for, recover, sell, buy, collect, forgive, receive, and hold money, debts, dues, commercial paper, checks, drafts, accounts, deposits, legacies, bequests, devises, notes, interests, stocks, bonds, certificates of deposit, annuities, pension and retirement benefits, insurance proceeds, any and all documents of title; choose in action, personal and real property, intangible and tangible property and property rights; and demand whatsoever,

liquidated or unliquidated, as now are or may become owned by, or due, owing, payable, or belonging to Grantor, or in which Grantor has or may hereafter acquire interest.

ii. Agent may use and take all lawful means and equitable and legal remedies, procedures, and writs in Grantor's name for the collection and recovery of the above; and may adjust, sell, compromise, and agree for the same; and to make, execute, and deliver for Grantor, on Grantor's behalf and in Grantor's name, all endorsements, acceptances, releases, receipts, or other sufficient discharges for the same.

b. Business.

i. Conduct, engage in and transact any lawful business of any nature on Grantor's behalf and in Grantor's name. Maintain, improve, invest, manage, insure, lease, or encumber; and in any manner deal with any real, personal, tangible, or intangible property, or any interest in them, that Grantor now owns or may acquire (or that an Agent hereunder may acquire), in Grantor's name and for Grantor's benefit, upon such terms and conditions as Agent shall deem proper.

ii. Conduct or participate in any business of any nature for Grantor and in Grantor's name; execute partnership agreements and amendments thereto; incorporate, reorganize, merge, consolidate, recapitalize, sell, liquidate, or dissolve any business; elect or employ officers, directors, and agents. Carry out the provisions of any agreement for the sale of any business interest or the stock therein; and exercise voting rights with respect to stock, either in person or by proxy; and exercise stock options.

c. Social Security and Government Benefits.

i. The Agent may apply to any governmental agency for any benefit or government obligation to which Grantor may be entitled, including but not limited to Social Security, Medicare, Medicaid, and Veterans benefits if applicable.

ii. The Agent may endorse any drafts or checks made payable to Grantor from any such agency and to serve as a representative payee for Social Security or other governmental payments. The Agent is expressly authorized to execute vouchers on Grantor's behalf for reimbursements properly payable to Grantor by the United States government or any agency thereof or any state agency. The Agent is expressly authorized to change Grantor's address for the purpose of receiving checks, mail, or other matters from the Social Security Administration or any other governmental agency.

d. Contract, Real Estate, and Other Matters.

i. The Agent may exercise or perform any act, power, duty, right, or obligation that Grantor now has, or may acquire, including the legal right, power, or capacity to exercise or perform in connection with, arising from, or relating to any person or property, real or personal, tangible or intangible, or matter whatsoever.

ii. This includes, without limiting the foregoing, the right to execute a deed or security agreement; to release a security agreement; to enter into a lease, option, mortgage or similar arrangement; to enter into a contract of sale and to sell or purchase any real, personal, tangible, or intangible property on Grantor's behalf.

iii. *Comment: Consider listing specific properties which the agent may sell or act upon. In addition, consider listing any property which you do not want the agent to sell or act upon.* The aforementioned powers shall apply, by way of example and not limitation, to the property (properties) located at *CLIENT-ADDRESS # and *OTHER PROPERTY.

e. Securities and Investments.

i. Make, receive, sign, endorse, acknowledge, deliver, and possess documents of title, bonds, debentures, checks, drafts, stocks, proxies, or warrants, relating to accounts or deposits, or certificates of deposit, other debts and obligations, and such other instruments in writing of whatever kind and nature as may be necessary or proper in the exercise of the rights and powers herein granted.

ii. Sell, or purchase any and all shares of stocks, bonds, or other securities now or later belonging to Grantor that may be issued by any association, trust, or corporation, whether private or public; and make, execute, and deliver any assignment, or assignments, of any such shares of stocks, bonds, or other securities.

f. Motor Vehicles.

Apply for any certificate of title, ownership, or license; endorse and transfer title regarding any automobile, motorcycle, or other motor vehicle or boat.

g. Legal Actions.

i. Settle, adjust, compromise, or submit to arbitration any accounts, claims, debts, demands, disputes, or other matters between Grantor and any other person or entity, or which concern any property, right, title, interest, or estate. Begin, prosecute, enforce, abandon, defend, or settle all claims or judicial or administrative proceedings.

ii. Execute and file documents to toll any statute of limitations. Grantor recognizes that the inclusion of the latter phrase may serve to prevent the tolling of a statute of limitations or other deadline which would otherwise be tolled pending Grantor's disability.

h. Retirement, IRA, and Other Benefit Plans and Beneficiary Designations.

i. *Comment: Be certain that you understand the consequences of this paragraph. Changing beneficiary designations on retirement and pension accounts can have profound tax consequences, can change the dispositive scheme of the largest asset in your estate.*

ii. Redeem, borrow, amend, cancel, pledge, surrender, alter, or change the beneficiary of any retirement, benefit, pension plan or other plan or account having a beneficiary designation form.

iii. However, this power may not be exercised by any agent who is a beneficiary (or spouse of a beneficiary) in a manner which disproportionately (as compared to the consequences of the beneficiary designation existing prior to the agent institute change) benefits such agent (or the spouse of such agent).

iv. Designate to the extent Grantor could one or more persons (including trusts) as designated beneficiaries of any such plan. Select any pay-out rate or election permitted to Grantor.

i. Employment of Accountants, Advisers, and Others.

Employ and compensate investment advisers, banks, accountants, expert witness, attorneys, real estate and other brokers, and other professionals or assistants to same, whom the Agent reasonably deems necessary. To cause such persons to prepare reports or analysis, and to act in reasonable reliance upon same, and to furnish any third party Agent believes necessary or appropriate such reports or analysis. There shall be no restriction on the Agent hiring or not hiring the advisers which grantor used.

j. Safe Deposit Box.

Have access at any time or times to any safe deposit box rented by Grantor, or for which Grantor is a co-tenant; remove all or any part of the contents thereof, and surrender or relinquish any safe deposit box. No institution in which any safe deposit box may be located shall incur any liability to Grantor or Grantor's estate as a result of permitting the Agent to exercise the powers herein granted.

k. Gifts.

The Agent shall not have any authority to make gifts.

l. Transfer of Property to Trust.

With respect to a revocable living trust for the benefit of Grantor the Agent may convey, transfer or assign any cash, real estate or other tangible or intangible property in which Grantor shall own any interest to the trustee or trustees of any trust that Grantor may have created during Grantor's lifetime, provided that such trust is subject to Grantor's power of revocation.

m. Postal Matters.

To execute any documents necessary or appropriate to securing a postal box, changing or correcting a postal mailing address, and making payments for same. By way of example and not limitation, this power shall expressly include the right to redirect mail from any former residence or post-office box to a new address or post-office box which the Agent reasonably believes will facilitate the management of Grantor's assets, tax, legal and other matters. Any third party, including but not limited to the United States government and any agency thereof, are directed to adhere to such requests of the Agent and are indemnified and held harmless for same.

n. Bond.

No bond or security of any kind shall be required in any jurisdiction of any Agent acting hereunder. If any bond is required by law, statute or rule of court, no sureties shall be required thereon. However, if any Agent deems it appropriate in such Agent's discretion to obtain a bond, such bond may be paid pursuant to the powers granted hereunder.

o. Insurance.

i. Make, receive, sign, endorse, acknowledge, deliver, and possess insurance policies. Execute any forms to change ownership or beneficiaries of any life insurance policy on Grantor's life.

ii. However, new beneficiaries may include only: Authorized Donees, a trust for which Authorized Donees are the primary beneficiaries, a corporation or partnership in which Grantor is a shareholder or partner, another shareholder or partner in a corporation or partnership in which Grantor is a shareholder or partner, Grantor's estate, or any trust of which Grantor is a grantor, trustee, or beneficiary.

**5. Powers Relating to Tax Matters.**

a. In addition to, and not by way of limitation upon, any other powers conferred upon Grantor's Agent herein, Grantor grants to the Agent full power and authority to do, take, and perform each and every act and thing which is reasonably required, proper, or necessary to be done in connection with the following:

b. Receiving and depositing to any of Grantor's bank or brokerage accounts any refund checks with respect to any tax filing. Preparing, signing, and filing joint or separate income tax returns, declarations, or estimated tax for any year or years, as provided in Treasury Regulation Section 1.6012-1(a)(5) and Treasury Regulation Section 25.60191(d), or otherwise.

c. Prepare, sign, and file joint or separate gift, or other tax returns, declarations, or estimated tax for any year or years, including by way of example, those with respect to gifts made by Grantor, or by Grantor's Agent on Grantor's behalf, for any year or years; consent to any gift and to utilize any gift-splitting provision or other tax election.

d. Dealing with the Internal Revenue Service and any federal, state, local, and foreign tax authority concerning any gift, estate, inheritance, income, or other tax, and any audit or investigation of same. Prepare, sign and file any claim for refund of any tax; execute any extension or waiver of tax.

e. The powers granted hereunder shall include, by way of example and not limitation, the power to do all acts that could be authorized by Grantor having properly executed a Form 2848, "Power of Attorney and Declaration of Representative," granting the broadest powers provided therein to the Agent, the power to represent Grantor in any federal, state, local, or foreign tax matter, to perform all acts that Grantor could perform relating thereto.

f. Prepare and file Form 56, "Notice Concerning Fiduciary Relationship," or any similar form, for purposes of directing tax and other correspondence, notices and information to a new address which the Agent deems appropriate. I expressly state that it is my intent that the Agent acting under this Power of Attorney shall be deemed a "fiduciary" for the purposes of the filing of Form 56, or any similar form.

**6. Compensation of Agent.** Any Agent or Alternate Agent hereunder shall be entitled to reasonable compensation for the services rendered. A bill estimating the hours spent, services performed and charges paid, shall be provided to any Alternate Agent acting hereunder with such Agent. It shall be deemed reasonable compensation for the Agent to be paid in a manner similar to that provided for a trustee to be compensated under applicable state law for the investment and liquid assets (e.g., excluding residential real estate, but including investment real estate if any) that the Agent has authority over. In the event of a short term flare-up, exacerbation or other emergency in which the Agent shall act in an emergent basis for a short period of time Grantor recognizes that compensation reflective of the time and effort over that short duration may be more reasonable.

**7. Cooperation With Health Care Agent.**

a. If Grantor has executed a separate Living Will, Health Care Proxy, or Durable Power of Attorney For Medical Decisions, or a similar form or document appointing any person or entity to serve as Grantor's health care agent, Grantor requests that Grantor's Agent appointed herein cooperate with such health care agent and keep such health care agent reasonably advised of any financial matters relating to Grantor's health care. To the extent possible, Agent should abide by such health care agent's decisions and actions concerning Grantor's health care and the matters covered in such documents named above, and should assist in providing financial resources reasonable and necessary to implement such decisions.

**8. Disability of Grantor.** This Power of Attorney shall not be affected by Grantor's subsequent disability as principal. Grantor does hereby so provide, it being Grantor's intention that all powers conferred upon the Agent herein shall remain at all times in full force and effect, notwithstanding Grantor's subsequent incapacity, disability, or any uncertainty with regard thereto.

**9. Third Party Reliance.**

a. Third parties may rely upon the representations of the Agent for all matters relating to any power granted to the Agent, and no person who may act in reliance upon the representations of the Agent or the authority granted to the Agent shall incur any liability to the Grantor or Grantor's estate as a result of permitting the Agent to exercise such power.

b. Any third party may rely on a duly executed counterpart of this instrument, or a copy thereof, as fully and completely as if such third party had received the original of this instrument. Any third party may rely on the authority of any Alternate Agent when such Alternate Agent presents an original executed copy of this Power of Attorney. Such third party need not request proof, other than an affidavit of the Alternate Agent, under oath, that any prior named Agent is unable or unwilling to serve in such capacity.

**10. Approval and Indemnification of Agent.** Grantor hereby approves and confirms all acts performed by Grantor's Agent on Grantor's behalf. Grantor hereby confirms all that the Agent shall do or cause to be done, by virtue of this Power of Attorney. The Grantor hereby agrees to indemnify and hold harmless the Agent for any actions taken, or not taken, by the Agent, when the Agent acted in good faith and was not guilty of fraud, gross negligence, or willful misconduct, only for matters in this document.

**11. Waiver of Conflicts for Agent and Successor Agent.** No Agent or successor Agent shall be disqualified from acting in such capacity as a result of having an interest in any assets, business, investment or endeavor in which Grantor also has an interest, and over which Agent may have authority to act, and may act upon, hereunder.

**12. HIPAA Provisions.**

a. The Grantor expressly authorizes any Agent or successor to request, obtain, receive, and inspect any and all information including private health information ("PHI") that encompasses solely Grantor's medical bills and related information ("Bills"), and to sign whatever authorizations for release of any Bills which may be required by Grantor's Agent or any third party providers or others, and to waive any rights Grantor may have for breach of confidentiality for the release of such information to the Agent or successor Agent.

b. In no event shall the provisions herein give the Agent or successor Agent hereunder any powers to make medical or health care decisions for me. These rights and powers are granted solely with respect to the implementation and conducting of the rights and powers granted herein, including by way of example and not limitation, reviewing and paying bills.

c. The Agent and Successor Agent shall be treated as Grantor would with regard to the use and dissemination of Grantor's Bills. This authority applies to any information governed by the Health Insurance Portability and Accountability Act of 1996 ("HIPAA"), 42 USC 130d and 45 CFR 160-164. Grantor specifically authorizes any physician, dentist, health care professional, medical provider, health plan, hospital, clinic, laboratory, pharmacy or other covered health care provider, any insurance company and the Medical Information Bureau Inc., or any other health care organization that has provided treatment or services to Grantor, or that has paid for or is seeking payment from Grantor for such services to give, disclose and release to the Grantor's Agent and successor Agent all of Grantor's Bills. The authority given to Grantor's Agent and successor Agents has no expiration date and shall expire only in the event that Grantor revokes the authority in writing and delivers it to Grantor's health care provider.

**13. Effective Date.**

a. The Grant to the Agent (not the Alternate Agents) shall take effect on the date hereof.

b. The Grant to an Alternate Agent shall take effect only in the event that the prior named Agent or Alternate Agent is unable or unwilling to Act.

**14. Construction.**

a. This instrument is to be construed and interpreted as a durable general power of attorney. The enumeration of specific items, rights, acts, or powers herein is not intended to nor does it limit or restrict, and is not to be construed or interpreted as limiting or restricting, the general powers herein granted to the Agent.

b. Should any provision or power in this document not be enforceable, such enforceability shall not affect the enforceability of the rest of this document. Any such provision is not enforceable shall be deemed severable and all other provisions shall remain enforceable and shall be interpreted in a manner that as closely as feasible implements Grantor's original intent hereunder.

c. Any references to the "Code" or any Sections of the Code are references to the Internal Revenue Code of 1986 and shall include any successor or amended Code, statute, or applicable Treasury Regulation.

d. Captions, titles, and section numbers (and letter designations) are inserted for convenience only and should not be read to broaden or limit the scope of any provision. Gender, singular or plural, shall be interpreted as the context requires.

### 15. State Law.

a. This instrument is executed in the state of *STATE-EXECUTION, but and is delivered in the state of *STATENAME ("State"), and the laws of *STATENAME shall govern all questions as to the validity of this power and the construction of its provisions. It is Grantor's intention, however, that this power of attorney be exercisable in any other state or jurisdiction in which Grantor may at any time have property, business, or other dealings. The Agent is, notwithstanding anything herein to the contrary, granted the right to exercise any of the rights and powers available under the laws of the State.

### 16. Signature.

a. **IN WITNESS WHEREOF,** I have hereunto set my hand and seal this *DAY of *MONTH, *YEAR, acknowledging that I have read and understood the powers and rights herein granted and that I voluntarily chose to make the Grant.

Grantor/Principal

_____

*CLIENTNAME

Witness 1:    Name: _____

              Address: _____

              Signature: _____

Witness 2:    Name: _____

              Address: _____

              Signature: _____

State of *STATE-EXECUTION

                                        SS:

County of *COUNTYNAME

On this *DAY of *MONTH, *YEAR, I, a Notary Public in the State of *STATE-EXECUTION, certify that before me personally appeared *CLIENTNAME, who resides at *CLIENT-ADDRESS, and who I am satisfied based on presentation of a *STATENAME driver's license, is the person named in and who executed the within Power of Attorney, and who acknowledged under oath, and to my satisfaction, that the execution of the Power of Attorney by Grantor was done voluntarily for the uses and purposes therein expressed, and that Grantor, signed, sealed, and delivered the Power of Attorney as Grantor's act and deed. The execution of this Power of Attorney by the Grantor was done in my presence and in the presence of both witnesses above, each of whom signed their names in my presence and in Grantor's presence.

_____

Notary Public, State of *STATE-EXECUTION

My commission expires on: _____ ___, 20___

## CHAPTER 7

# Ensuring Access to Your Medical Records
## HIPAA

## Introduction to HIPAA

"HIPAA" IS THE ACRONYM FOR THE Health Insurance Portability and Accountability Act of 1996. HIPAA, as amended (it takes multiple efforts to perfect such complexity), protects your rights to your medical information, legally designated as "protected health information" or "PHI." HIPAA was enacted to ensure your access to your medical information while simultaneously preventing others who should not have access to it from obtaining it. HIPAA rules have broad implications affecting a wide range of personal, estate planning, and business transactions.

### WHY HIPAA MATTERS

HIPAA regulations determine how and to whom your medical information should be disclosed, and it is vitally important to understand these regulations and how they might affect you and people who have a vested interest in your health care. If, for example, you have a flare-up or go for surgery, does your daughter-in-law have the right to see your patient chart to monitor your care? If you're a trustee on your own revocable living trust, can your successor trustee take over in the event you deteriorate to the point where you cannot reasonably continue to serve as your own trustee? And does this individual have the right to view any medical information about you? If you have a partner in an accounting practice, chances are you and your partner may have discussed contingency plans if your health or cognitive issues reach a level that makes it necessary for your partner to take over the practice. If your health status deteriorates, how can your partner obtain the requisite physician letter mandated in your shareholders' agreement to demonstrate your incompetence and thus trigger the buy-out of your interests? HIPAA needs to be addressed in all of these and many other common situations.

# WHAT A MEDICAL PROVIDER ("COVERED ENTITY") MUST DO TO PROTECT YOU

Despite our society's current obsession with political correctness, most people with a chronic illness (or a loved one with a chronic illness) know the harsh non-PC reality of living in a world that is not always understanding or tolerant of chronic illness and those who are affected by it. Many people, in fact, including employers and others who may have the power to affect your life and livelihood can be ignorant, even antagonistic, to those with disabilities or health challenges. For this reason alone, you are not likely to want your private medical information disclosed, and you have the right to restrict disclosure. Often you'll find when someone has a legitimate need to access some of your health information the forms they provide you to authorize them to do so are very overbroad. In many cases, reasonably restricting the information you are giving them access to, while ensuring they can get what they reasonably need, is feasible, if you ask. Some of the following discussion will provide you some background understanding of these issues.

Under HIPAA regulations, any organization (health plan, health care provider, or health clearinghouse) that routinely handles private health information in any capacity is probably characterized as a "covered entity" and all covered entities must provide information to their patients about their privacy rights and how their PHI can be used (notice of privacy practices). A covered entity must adopt clear and appropriate privacy policies and procedures for its practice, hospital, or plan. It must train its workforce to understand its privacy procedures and must designate a privacy officer responsible for ensuring that privacy procedures are adopted and followed. A covered entity must also adopt adequate security procedures for patient records containing individually identifiable private health information. Because medical practices fall under the classification of covered entity, even your doctor cannot disclose your health status to your employer or others without your authorization.

## WHEN INFORMATION CAN BE DISCLOSED

Your otherwise protected health information should be disclosed for medical treatment, payment, and health care operations (no authorization or release is needed). Your medical information should be disclosed to you at your request. This is important because prior to HIPAA, a patchwork of state and local rules governed the release of health information, and your right to access your own medical records was not always assured. Your HIPAA personal representative (an agent selected by you and discussed in detail below) should also have access to your protected health information. A court can also order disclosure of your medical information. This can occur if, for example, someone tries to have a guardian appointed for you (a process you can likely avoid by taking the planning precautions in this book).

## WHEN INFORMATION MAY NOT BE DISCLOSED

If your physician, neurologist, or other health care professional believes that the disclosure of your health information might endanger your life, jeopardize your physical safety, or cause you or another person (e.g., someone else mentioned in your records) substantial harm, they can refuse in their professional judgment to disclose the information.

## WHAT INFORMATION CAN BE DISCLOSED

Not all information has to be disclosed. Medical providers are only supposed to disclose the minimum information necessary to achieve the purpose of the requested disclosure. This can be an important safeguard of your confidentiality, but it might also prove to be a hindrance to your HIPAA personal representative. In part, what is disclosed will depend on the policies of the particular physician (or more broadly, the covered entity, which might be the entire medical practice). What is disclosed will also depend on the language you put in the legal documents authorizing someone to obtain disclosure of your medical records. To protect and limit the scope of what is disclosed, you should clearly delineate in any document you execute the specific purpose of the disclosure and what information should not be disclosed. Consider your unique situation and evolving circumstances when deciding what should, or should not, be disclosed.

EXAMPLE

If you are seeking to ensure that one of your adult children can help you with medical decisions, you may expressly want no limits imposed on what access they have to your health information. In such a situation, a broad authorization to release all of your protected health information could be stated. Be careful with "standard" authorization forms. Just like the issues discussed in the preceding chapter on "standard" powers of attorney, generic forms related to health information can be quite unreasonable. Standard forms for the release of your private health information may be too broad or too narrow, depending on your objectives. In some instances you may want extremely narrow disclosures. For example, assume that you are a nurse and that the medical practice you work for wants assurance that your COPD won't negatively affect your ability to work. It is certainly reasonable for your colleagues to receive a letter from your pulmonologist that your illness won't adversely affect your practicing. On the other hand, an excessively broad grant of authority to access your medical information could result in disclosures of personal information way beyond what is necessary and appropriate. You certainly don't want anyone in the office having the leeway to request records from your psychotherapist. So to avoid abuses of your privacy, any document you sign should appropriately and reasonably restrict who should have access to your information and what information should be disclosed. The main reason this doesn't happen is that frequently those needing access to medical information use a broad standard form that is available, and most people requested to sign such an authorization assume that it's "standard" and just sign it. Read before you sign anything.

## HOW TO GET INFORMATION DISCLOSED

As explained above, a medical provider ("covered entity") cannot disclose your protected health information (PHI) without your authorization. There are some exceptions to this policy, but HIPAA ensures that general access to your health information is strictly limited. You, as a patient, have the right to authorize the release of your PHI. An individual designated as your HIPAA "personal representative" (this is a phrase that is defined in the law) can also authorize the release of your PHI, but this authorization is governed by specific requirements. In order for the person you designate as your agent to have access to your medical records, the following requirements must be met.

❖     *Writing.* The authorization should be in writing. It should expressly state that your consent is voluntary and that your treatment, payment, and health plan eligibility should not be affected whether or not you authorize the release of information.

❖    *What.* The authorization should describe the health information to be disclosed, whether such information includes your entire medical record or only specified components of that record. You might specify that only those medical records pertaining to certain dates or time periods be released. If you wish alcohol and drug treatment, HIV testing, and mental health information released (or not released), the document you sign should expressly say this. The HIPAA paradigm is that only as much information should be disclosed as necessary. However, it is unreasonable to expect a medical provider to determine what constitutes "necessary" or "unnecessary" for every patient, so the authorization you sign should be explicit.

❖    *Who.* Which medical provider should make the disclosure? This could be a specific pulmonologist, internist, psychologist, physician, or hospital. Alternatively, it could be a list of several medical care providers or a category of providers. For example, "any physicians, hospitals, or other medical providers who have provided treatment, other medical services or payment for same, from June 1, 2004, through and including the date of this Authorization." How broad or narrow you make the list depends on what your goal is and who you are naming as your HIPAA representative.

❖    *Term.* When does the authorization to disclose PHI expire? This could be "upon a child attaining age twenty-one," which might suffice for a minor's care. It could be "two years from the signing of the authorization," which should be more than adequate for a life insurance application. "Upon the conclusion of the court case of XX versus YY, Docket No. _____" may suffice for a litigation matter, although issues of appeals, etc., might dictate the parameters to be set. "One year from death" might be used in a health care proxy to ensure your agent has access to your records while you are alive as well as for evaluation of postdeath records without the need to qualify as the executor of your estate. If COPD or another illness you have will impact your competency or eventually result in your being incapacitated, you might want to expressly provide that the grant of authority will not lapse. If the authorization involves a trustee, it might be "so long as serving as trustee of the [identify trust]."

❖    *Revocation.* A revocation is a statement that you retain the right to revoke any authorization to disclose your PHI. Any revocation, however, is not binding on a medical provider until received. This minimizes the extent of a provider's liability for disclosing information based on an authorization held prior to the revocation. Obviously, if in the future your disease progresses to the point of your having a significant cognitive impairment, at some point you might lack the capacity to revoke the authorization.

❖   *Redisclosure.* The release may state that certain information, such as HIV testing results, cannot be disclosed by the person receiving it. However, the release should also acknowledge that once other information is disclosed, it may thereafter be redisclosed by the person receiving it without violating the HIPAA safeguards.

❖   *Purpose.* The purpose for the disclosure should be explained. This might be limited to the minimum information to determine whether you have the ability to function as a trustee or should be replaced, or only the information necessary to underwrite you for life insurance. However, it is quite likely that you will wish to grant a trusted friend or family member the right to monitor your care throughout your illness, so a broad authorization may be more appropriate in that instance.

❖   *Signer.* If you are signing the authorization, the signature line should merely state that you are the patient. If, however, another person is signing for you, the authorization should state that signatory qualifies as your personal representative under HIPAA, that he or she has authority to make health care decisions for you (e.g., the agent under your health care proxy), and a brief note defining the scope of the representative's authority. It might also be advisable to indicate the source of this person's authority to be your HIPAA representative. For an adult or emancipated minor, this could be a health care proxy, court appointment as guardian, or an agent under your general power of attorney. Arguably, it could be a trustee under a trust agreement, depending on the terms of the trust. For a minor patient, it might be the signer's position as parent or guardian. For an estate, it would most likely be the signer's role as executor.

## MENTAL HEALTH INFORMATION

Psychotherapy notes are not required to be released unless you expressly authorize them to be released. But as cautioned above, there is no such thing as a "standard" form. You need to read what you are requested to sign and if it is unacceptable to you, modify it and initial the changes. The challenge you will face in many cases is that whoever is requesting you to sign a release will be adamant that it is a "standard" and "required" form.

Persist and in many cases reasonable modifications may be agreeable. If they aren't, consider your options (maybe it is a sign of the lack of attention and consideration that might motivate you to change to a different provider).

## EMPOWERING AN AGENT TO RELEASE YOUR PHI

There are myriad reasons you might want to have an agent or personal representative act on your behalf with regard to HIPAA matters. This agent can act with the same authority as if he or she were standing in your shoes, but this person must be chosen with care and with a full understanding of legal requirements that must be met when selecting this person. Here's what the law says: "In general, the scope of the personal representative's authority to act for the individual under the Privacy Rule derives from his or her authority under applicable law to make health care decisions for the individual." The definition is quite nettlesome. If a person has broad authority to make health care decisions for another person, such as a parent for a minor child, or a legal guardian for an incompetent adult, that person should generally be treated as stepping into the shoes of the minor or ward for HIPAA purposes. Exceptions may apply in instances of abuse or if state law provides to the contrary. "Where the authority to act for the individual is limited, or specific to particular health care decisions, the personal representative is to be treated as the individual only with respect to protected health information that is relevant to the representation."

Can your agent under your power of attorney be your personal representative? Not necessarily. Your agent under your financial power of attorney is generally not empowered to make health care-related decisions. Although paying medical bills may constitute making decisions related to health care, it may not be enough because this person's ability to obtain PHI will be limited to those matters pertaining to paying medical bills. How broad of a medical decision-making authority should an agent under your power of attorney be granted? And at what point might your financial agent's authority conflict with your health care agent's? For example, if your financial agent is to make the financial decisions as to which health care facility to pay for, will the agent be entitled to all of the information required to make that decision? As discussed in the preceding chapter, you probably won't want your financial agent to dictate health care decisions by controlling the payment of matters that should remain within the purview of your health care agent. So you don't want to inadvertently make the HIPAA and related language in your financial power so broad that you undermine the goal of having a separate health care agent make health related decisions.

## FIDUCIARIES

The term "fiduciary" means a person who is serving in a position of trust. This includes agents under your power of attorney and health proxy, as well as your trustee (the person who manages a trust you set up) and your executor (the person who manages your estate when you die). After your death, it is the executor of your estate who automatically becomes your HIPAA personal representative and has the authority to act on your behalf concerning any protected health information.

If you set up a revocable living trust to protect yourself, your trustee and successor trustees will need access to your medical records to pay medical bills and handle other administrative matters. If the same people are also named as agents under your health care proxy to make health care decisions, there should be no problem in doing so. If they are not (which is common; the people named as trustees are usually selected for their business and investment acumen), then the same issues and steps discussed in the preceding section as to how your agent under your power of attorney would deal with HIPAA would apply to your fiduciaries as well.

## CHAPTER SUMMARY

HIPAA affects a broad range of personal, financial, health care, and estate planning transactions. Almost every key estate document, and many important business documents, need to address HIPAA disclosure issues to ensure that various mechanisms (succession of fiduciaries, determinations of disability, etc.) can be triggered. The issues are quite complex but are an important part of planning for your care and future.

**Caution:** The HIPAA authorization and release form on the following pages is merely an illustration and you must discuss the appropriate form to use with an attorney in your state.

## HIPAA AUTHORIZATION AND RELEASE FORM

I, *CLIENT NAME (Social Security Number: *SOCIAL SEC #), residing at *CLIENT ADDRESS, being of the age of majority under the laws of *STATE NAME, do hereby declare as follows:

1. **Appointment of Agent**. I hereby make, constitute, and appoint ("Grant") *AGENT 1 NAME, residing at or doing business at *AGENT 1 ADDRESS to be my agent under the Health Insurance Portability and Accountability Act of 1996, 42 USC 130d and 45 CFR 160–164, and in particular its 2003 Privacy Regulations ("HIPAA") ("Agent").

### 2. Powers of Agent.

i. My agent shall be treated as I would with regard to the use and dissemination of my individually identifiable health information and medical records.

ii. This authority applies to any information governed by the HIPAA rules and regulations. I specifically authorize any health plan, physician, dentist, health care professional, hospital, clinic, laboratory, pharmacy, medical facility, insurance company and the Medical Information Bureau Inc., or any other health care organization that has provided payment, treatment or services to me or on my behalf or that has paid for or is seeking payment from me for such services (my "Provider") to give, disclose and release to my Agent all of my individually identifiable health information and medical records regarding any past, present or future medical matter, including but not limited to records as to my mental health condition including but not limited to all information relating to the diagnosis and treatment of mental illness and the use of alcohol or drugs. This authorization specifically includes psychotherapy notes. "Psychotherapy notes" means notes recorded (in any medium) by a health care provider who is a mental health professional documenting or analyzing the contents of conversation during a private counseling session or a group, joint, or family counseling session and that are separate from the rest of my medical records. *Caution: This is a broad provision that grants access to psychotherapy and other personal records. This is an example of the type of language you may wish to limit or eliminate.*

iii. I specifically authorize the release of medication prescription and monitoring, counseling session start and stop times, the modalities and frequencies of treatment furnished, results of clinical tests, and any summary of the following items: diagnosis, functional status, the treatment plan, symptoms, prognosis, and progress to date.

iv. The purpose of this Release is to address my current and future care in light of the current and potential future impact of my chronic illness, I have expressly made this grant of authority to the agents listed broad in terms of Protected Health Information they can access, the medical providers including covered entities that should disclose information to my agent, and the duration of this authorization. I expressly intend that this grant continue in such broad capacity if I shall in the future be incapacitated.

v. This Authorization is expressly made valid for all documents held by any medical providers including any covered entity that has or shall hereafter provided me with medical or related or ancillary care. *Caution: This is a broad provision that grants access to records of every medical provider. This is an example of the type of language you may wish to limit or eliminate.*

3. **Prior Agreements with Providers**. The authority given to my Agent by this Authorization shall supersede any prior agreement I have made to restrict my personal health information and unless specifically noted, and I instruct my Providers to release and disclose to my Agent my entire medical record without restriction as set forth in this Authorization.

4. **Indemnification**. All persons and entities shall not incur any liability to me or my estate as a result of permitting my Agent access to any information or to exercise any power relating to my medical condition. I hereby agree to indemnify and hold harmless any such third party from and against any and all claims that may arise against such third party by reason of such third party having relied on the provisions of this instrument.

**5. Copies of Document**. A copy, facsimile, and PDF of this Authorization are as valid as the original.

**6. Competency to Execute Document**. I understand the full import of this document and I am emotionally and mentally competent to execute it.

**7. Disability Does Not Affect Validity of this Document**. This Authorization shall not, to the extent permitted by applicable law, be affected by my disability as principal, and I do hereby so provide, it being my intention that all powers conferred upon my Agent herein or any substitute designated by me shall remain at all times in full force and effect, notwithstanding my incapacity, disability, or any uncertainty with regard thereto. This provision shall be interpreted in the broadest terms so as to remain in effect throughout my disability to the fullest extent provided for under the laws of state in which it is executed. Because I presently have a chronic illness for which there is no known cure, I recognize that the grant of authority hereunder will be for the duration of my lifetime. I understand and expressly reaffirm the broad time horizon for this document.

**8. Construction and Interpretation of this Document**. This instrument is to be construed and interpreted as a HIPAA release authorization for medical, health care and related matters. The enumeration of specific items, rights, acts or powers herein is not intended to, nor does it limit or restrict, and is not to be construed or interpreted as limiting or restricting the general powers herein granted to said Agent. This instrument is executed and delivered in the state indicated below, and the laws of the state of shall govern all questions as to the validity of this power and the construction of its provisions. Should any provisions or power in this document not be enforceable, such enforceability shall not affect the enforceability of the rest of this document. Should this grant be prohibited by any law presently existing or hereinafter enacted, it is my specific desire that such grant be interpreted in the broadest manner permitted by such law, and that in the event such grant is prohibited, that every other provision of this Authorization shall remain fully valid and enforceable.

**9. Effective Date**. This Authorization shall be effective as of the date it is executed.

**10. No Time Limit; Duration.**

a. I have considered the possibility of limiting the effectiveness of this instrument to a fixed period of time from the date hereof but have intentionally chosen not to do so.

b. I have decided that it shall remain in full force and effect for as long as I may live unless terminated as provided below.

c. Unless this Authorization is revoked in writing by me, with actual delivery of said revocation to the person or entity in question, it shall continue to be in force and effect and shall expressly not expire.

**11. Revocation**. I understand that a revocation is not effective to the extent that any of my Providers have relied on this.

**12. Redisclosure**. I understand that any information that is disclosed pursuant to this authorization may be re-disclosed and no longer covered by federal rules governing privacy and confidentiality of health information.

**13. Termination.**
a. This Authorization shall be modified or terminated, as the case may be, upon my executing a termination document or upon my executing a written notice of modification or termination and such Agent's receipt of same. I recognize that should I lack the competency to revoke this Authorization, at that future point in time this Authorization will not be able to be revoked. I expressly intend this result and request that any medical provider respect this wish.

b. As to any Provider, this Authorization shall be modified or terminated, as the case may be, upon such Provider receiving actual notice of a modification or termination.

IN WITNESS WHEREOF, I have hereunto set my hand and seal this *MONTH *DAY, *YEAR.

_____
*CLIENT NAME

Witness: _____

State of *STATE-EXECUTION

County of *COUNTY NAME

BE IT REMEMBERED, that on this *MONTH *DAY, *YEAR, before me, the subscriber, a notary of the State of *STATE-EXECUTION, personally appeared *CLIENT NAME who, I am satisfied after inspection of *STATE NAME #driver's license, is the principal mention in, and who executed the above HIPAA Authorization and Release and acknowledged that he or she signed, sealed and delivered the same as his or her act and deed, that he or she appeared to be of sound mind and not under any duress, fraud or undue influence, and for the uses and purposes therein expressed.

_____
Notary Signature

CHAPTER **8**

# YOUR HEALTH CARE PROXY AND LIVING WILL

## DESIGNATING SOMEONE TO MAKE HEALTH CARE DECISIONS FOR YOU

## INTRODUCTION TO HEALTH CARE PROXIES AND LIVING WILLS

A HEALTH CARE PROXY IS A LEGAL DOCUMENT in which you designate a trusted person (agent) to make health care decisions for you if you are unable to do so yourself because of illness or disability. A living will is a statement that defines your health care wishes. Although the two documents are integrally related, having them prepared and executed as independent documents may facilitate their use in many instances. Some health care providers prefer a health care proxy so that they can have your named agent execute documents confirming health care decisions. In other situations, hospitals or medical facilities may insist on a living will simply because of their policies. In many instances, a detailed personalized explanation of your health care wishes, as provided by a living will, may be essential to provide guidance to those making decisions for you.

The focus of the health care proxy is for you to appoint someone as your agent to make health care decisions. Some states do not afford the same recognition to a living will as they do to a health care proxy. In those states, the health care proxy empowering your agent will be the only document with legal weight. Nevertheless, the personal details in your living will remain an important source of insight into your wishes. No matter which document you use to indicate your health care decisions, it should be prepared in a manner that presents "clear and convincing" proof of your wishes. Vague and general statements as to "no heroic measures" and the like, which are typically used in many boilerplate living wills may not suffice. This is especially dangerous for anyone living with COPD, as will be explained in greater detail below. You should never sign "standard" forms without carefully reading and understanding the implications to you and your COPD. Have each of the documents witnessed and notarized separately. The laws differ from state to state so you want to be sure that whatever formalities of signature are used comply with your state's laws. It may be advisable to even do more than your state law requires so you'll be less likely to have an issue if you have an acute health situation you have to deal with while you are traveling in another state.

The safest approach is for you to sign both a living will and a health care proxy, but in all cases only after making certain that your wishes are clearly and convincingly stated. To be "clear and convincing" will often require you to elaborate on the standard language many forms contain. This is especially important in light of the impact of your health status. You should really endeavor to custom tailor the statements in your living will and health care proxy so that they clearly show how your experience of COPD affects your directives.

The health care proxy (power of attorney for medical directives) provides a mechanism for decisions to be made by your chosen representatives if, when, and where the need exists. It is impossible to foresee every possible future illness or every possible treatment your doctors may prescribe no matter how "clear and convincing" you try to make the language in your document. By appointing a person to act on your behalf, you ensure that these decisions can be made based on your condition at a given time, and that the decisions about available medical procedures and recommendations are made in accordance with your wishes.

### EXAMPLE

You might have a very specific view of pain relief and how this relates to your illness. You may also have views on "heroic medical efforts" or hospice care that differ (modestly or substantially) from the standard language and explanations that most attorneys normally use to define them. Most people signing these documents have no idea what, if any, health issues may affect them in the future, and this is why most forms are so generic. For people with COPD, the paradigm is different. You likely have significant knowledge of your current condition and most likely have a pretty good idea about likely future health issues. Use this knowledge to tailor standard forms. Don't accept generic language that really doesn't address your concerns.

It is also important to make room for hope in your documents. There is fascinating, cutting-edge research being conducted that may well result in a breakthrough for COPD. In the event a significant discovery occurs, it is important for your agent to have the flexibility to react and change decisions made before then.

## IMPORTANCE OF YOUR LIVING WILL

A living will is one of the most important and personal documents that you will ever sign. It is also one of the most controversial, misunderstood, and misapplied legal documents. As with too many important decisions, living wills have become a "quick fix" that seldom addresses everything that should be addressed. Here are some of the mistakes that people make with living wills:

❖     Sign a quick one-page standard form with your lawyer and your worries are over. Unfortunately, important legal, financial, religious, and medical issues will not be addressed unless you are proactive.

❖     An even worse approach is to use a form you purchase on the Internet. Most of these forms are so generic, or so poorly drafted, that extreme caution is in order. Yes, they are less costly and you don't need to see a lawyer, but you wouldn't handle your own medical care based on a bit of online research, and legal planning is no less sophisticated.

❖     The worst approach of all is to sign a form a hospital employee hands you when you are admitted because you've taken no action in advance. Regardless of the quality of a hospital-provided form, signing a document during the chaos and stress of an emergency hospital admission is never wise.

The information provided below will guide you through the process of properly communicating your wishes. It will explain how you can obtain the best protection and comfort from your living will and health care proxy in a simple and practical manner. It will also give you ideas how to tailor these documents to reflect some of the unique issues created by your special situation. There are various methods of communicating your wishes to the attorney you are working with, and this process should begin with identifying questions or concerns you may have. With this attention to detail, your attorney can more thoroughly and economically assist you in the preparation of a comprehensive living will and health care proxy. Once this process is completed, the final forms will help you inform and guide your family, loved ones, and health care providers in making many vital medical decisions. Your documents should minimize the legal interference and complications of carrying out your wishes.

## WHY YOU NEED A LIVING WILL AND HEALTH CARE PROXY

Deciding how you should be cared for in the event of a medical crisis related to your chronic illness, the deterioration of your condition, or even an unrelated medical event, is extraordinarily difficult and emotional. The importance of making your wishes about health care treatment known in the event you are unable to communicate your decisions when you are gravely ill has become an integral part of estate and personal planning for everyone. Without advance preparation, living wills, and health care proxies (the documents used to communicate your health care wishes), your desires may not be carried out. Without proper documentation, your family or loved ones may face gut-wrenching decisions about your care. There is no solace to be found in knowing what you would have wanted and not being able to act (or not act) on that knowledge.

In some cases, family members and loved ones do not know what you want, and this makes decision making even more difficult. Thinking about and discussing illness can never be a pleasant or easy matter. However, your failure to provide your loved ones with guidance now, while you are able to, may cause them to have to second-guess what you would have wanted done. This will be a far more difficult and emotionally traumatic task for them.

It is thus essential to communicate guidelines, in writing, about how you want to be cared for in the event of a medical emergency, deterioration of your condition (whether anticipated or unexpected), or a terminal illness. They must have the legal authority to do so. Not completing this admittedly unpleasant process now can only create more costs, difficulties, and unpleasantness later—for you and your loved ones. Your personal goals will be compromised and you may spend the final months or years of your life in agony or confronting quality-of-life issues that are unacceptable.

If you do not address living will and related health care issues now, you leave yourself open to having doctors, courts, or others making decisions for you, often with results that you would not have chosen. Remember you have a distinct advantage over those people who do not know what lies ahead because your knowledge about your current illness and the course it may take can help you make choices about many of the medical issues that will affect you in the future.

## WHY A COMPREHENSIVE DOCUMENT IS IMPORTANT

The kind of document recommended in this discussion is more comprehensive than what is provided in many of the commercial forms you can purchase in office supply stores or obtain from various organizations. Often the commercial forms are limited to simple instructions such as "pulling the plug" in the event of a terminal illness. This language can be particularly dangerous with COPD. With COPD you may have a nearly normal life expectancy of many decades. The simplistic language in many standard forms might effectively imply that you don't want any medical intervention, even in the present, hopefully something that does not conform with your wishes in the least. Directives in a standard form might imply no further care or intervention should be provided. If you want protection against this kind of ambiguity and lack of precision, you need a much more comprehensive document.

The form you use must address your personal needs and concerns, not simply a generic list of choices. Your personal preferences, religious concerns, family, and other personal relationships should all be considered.

## COPD IMPACTS HEALTH CARE PROXIES AND LIVING WILLS

COPD, although progressive, is also commonly marked by flare-ups or exacerbations. An acute respiratory flare-up may require hospitalization. Many living with COPD are advised to have in place emergency plans to address a crisis, for example, they cannot breath and need to be rushed to the hospital. A properly prepared, and readily accessible, health proxy and living will can serve an important role in facilitating that preparedness.

Living with COPD makes that emergency planning real, not hypothetical. While the steps are simple, without focusing on tailoring them for COPD you may not achieve the protections desired. Both you and your agent should have an accessible copy of your living will, health care proxy (medical power of attorney), and HIPAA release (preceding chapter) with the emergency documentation you keep at the ready, typically in your home. If you travel, it might be advisable that an extra set of original documents be prepared for traveling to enable you not to worry about leaving the home emergency documents elsewhere. Similarly if you have vacation property you frequent, an extra set of originals for that location may be useful as well.

These are simple steps, but for anyone living with COPD the anxiety of having left critical emergency legal documents elsewhere could be more than an inconvenience. When anyone experiences severe anxiety, oxygen requirements are increased. For someone living with COPD this could trigger further and more serious complications. So preparedness may, in itself, lessen the likelihood of an emergency occurring.

## EXPERIMENTAL OR COSTLY MEDICAL PROCEDURES

Someone living with COPD may be desirous of risking experimental medical procedures now or in the future. Your living will and health care proxy should reflect these wishes. There may also be costs associated with some approved medical treatments that insurance might not cover, as well as non approved or experimental medical treatment. For example, there is an alpha-1 replacement for those living with alpha-1 antitrypsin deficiency. Would you wish to incur such a cost? The following is illustrative language that might be added to a revocable trust:

> "Grantor is aware that this trust agreement authorizes the Trustee to pay for Grantor's medical and other health care expenses. Grantor further authorizes and directs the Trustee to pay for any medical procedure or drug, regardless of the cost, as well as for any experimental, unproven, alternative or other medical procedures, drug therapies or other medical therapies which [are authorized by Grantor's health care proxy] or [may assist Grantor in consultation with the medical specialists attending Grantor from time to time]."

# INTUBATION PROVISIONS IN HEALTH CARE PROXIES

**Example**: A typical form or boilerplate living will or health proxy provision might provide as follows:

> I direct all physicians and medical facilities in whose care I may be, and my family and all those concerned with my care, to refrain from and cease extraordinary or heroic life sustaining treatments (i.e., that the following be considered heroic) including, without limitation, antibiotics, pulmonary resuscitation, ventilation, intubation, or other respiratory support.

Even if such language might be acceptable to a client with no respiratory issues (that is not suggested), it would be an unworkable course for anyone with COPD. For many with COPD, supplemental oxygen is essential. Many living with COPD utilize both stationary or base oxygen support systems and portable oxygen systems. A stationary system, for example, may include a liquid oxygen container, a concentrator with an electric motor, an electronic demand valve, tubing, and so forth. A face mask or even transtracheal catheter (a tube supplying oxygen into the windpipe) may be used to deliver the oxygen to you. These oxygen delivery systems may be used regularly by the person with COPD who may, with the assistance of these devices, maintain a rather ordinary and active life. Yet, the boilerplate living will clause above provides that ventilation, intubation, and respiratory support are heroic measures to be avoided. Ventilation is the act of breathing — oxygen going in and out. Intubation is inserting a breathing tube permitting someone to be connected to a respirator if they cannot breathe themselves. You could be sitting at the document execution meeting in your lawyer's office signing a document preventing the same device you are using while at the meeting! Care must be taken by estate planning practitioners to carefully review any boilerplate language concerning intubation, heroic measures, and the like, and ensure that it is appropriate and reasonable for you. Some standard provisions will not be.

Similarly, the characterization of antibiotics as a heroic measure may also be inappropriate for anyone with COPD. As explained earlier a common symptom of COPD, especially those with chronic bronchitis, is increased and thickened secretions that often become infected ("purulent"). Characterizing antibiotics, which may be a regular part of your medical regimen, as "heroic" may be inappropriate and if acted upon (i.e., consider to be heroic) your death knell.

A modicum of background might be helpful to estate planners endeavoring to guide you in these life-determining decisions. While certainly, since you have known health issues you should be encouraged to discuss end-of-life decisions with your physicians and social worker, counsel needs some understanding in order to draft the provisions memorializing the your wishes. If there is an emergency with breathing, for example, pneumonia (you cannot breathe), medical providers will insert a breathing tube into your trachea (windpipe) and put you on a ventilator. This is referred to as intubation. The ventilator will breathe for you while efforts are made to treat the underlying problem. For example, antibiotics and steroids may be introduced. Breathing tubes only stay in place for a short duration, for example, a week, which may be viewed as a long time. If there is no short-term hope to wean you off the ventilator, the decision may be made to electively perform a "tracheotomy," which is to surgically provide an airway. This is also referred to as an "ostomy." Tracheotomies are easier to care for, and are more comfortable for you then being intubated. Intubation requires that an endotracheal tube be inserted in your airway. A tracheotomy does not present the same risks of damage to you as an endotracheal tube. A tracheotomy is for purposes of longer term airway management. The weaning process from the ventilator can be done more slowly.

### EXAMPLE

Thomas Smith, age 58, has chronic emphysema but at present no other diseases. He has been a relatively compliant patient adhering to the regimen for his care. However, this past winter Thomas developed pneumonia. Without intervention Thomas may not survive the bout of pneumonia because of his already weakened lung function. However, the use of a respiratory machine may provide Thomas the ability to rest and recuperate while antibiotics are introduced to combat the pneumonia. As Thomas recovers there is every anticipation that he will be weaned from the respiratory machine and return to a relatively normal life. The sample boilerplate heroic measures clause could prohibit the use of both antibiotics and the breathing machine.

As stated, the decision making needs to be tailored to your situation. The example above is not intended to suggest that anyone living with COPD should utilize a clause mandating ventilation, intubation, and so on. The example above is an acute event that requires life support for Thomas to live, and with those measures it would appear likely that he would survive and have some quality of life. While certainly there is no assurance of result in any acute medical situation, the key point is to contrast that with a more chronic end-stage scenario depicted below.

EXAMPLE

Jane Craymour, age 78, has chronic emphysema, end-stage ovarian cancer, and is in a generally weakened state of health as a result of a recent COPD flare-up. She is now living in an assisted living facility because it has become too difficult for her family to care for her. Jane's pulmonologist is concerned that a bout of pneumonia would likely be fatal in her weakened state. The social worker in the facility Jane is in encourages her to consult her attorney and put her affairs in order. In contrast to Thomas Smith in the preceding example, Jane believes that intubation and the use of a ventilator and similar measures should be viewed as heroic if she is admitted to a hospital on an emergency basis. The sample boilerplate heroic measures clause prohibiting general respiratory support measures (e.g., antibiotics) may still be inappropriate. At the assisted living facility, Jane may receive respiratory treatments consisting of lung medications such as Proventyl, Atrovent, and so on. These are given as inhalant respirator therapies. She might also receive chest physical therapy. Jane will likely want this skilled nursing level of care continued. However, Jane may wish to provide in her living will that she should not have invasive procedures. Jane might expressly wish to provide that she does not wish to be mechanically ventilated, which requires insertion of an endotracheal tube and being put on a ventilator.

Comparing and contrasting the two hypothetical situations above illustrate how at different stages of COPD you might wish different levels of care specified in your medical directives. But perhaps in all cases, language some standard forms use will be excessively and inappropriately restrictive.

## CHOOSING YOUR HEALTH CARE AGENT

Choosing whom to appoint as your agent can be very difficult. Many loved ones, however sensitive to your feelings, may simply not be able to make the very difficult decisions that might become necessary as your health deteriorates. Sadly, many people living with chronic illness discover that close family, rather than circling the wagons in support, head for the hills. This, obviously, limits your choices considerably and also suggests that you may have to think about appointing someone who is not part of your immediate family.

Another point that must be made here is that you should never name two or more people to make a joint decision. There are two important reasons for this, the most obvious being that making decisions in a crisis is difficult enough without having to make a decision with someone who may disagree with you. Furthermore, some state laws prohibit joint agents, which will make the appointment ineffectual. If you want to name two people to make decisions, name them sequentially (that is, the second only can serve if the first cannot). You can then add nonbinding language to the health care proxy suggesting, but not requiring, that all agents consult each other (if feasible) before acting. This recommendation might, in fact, be made in a separate letter of instruction, an approach that allows you to express your wishes without inviting unnecessary legal issues.

Do not necessarily assume that the person you select will be able to carry out your wishes. Some prospective agents may have religious, moral, or other personal reasons for not being willing to carry out certain wishes. For example, many people simply do not have the emotional composure to be able to "pull the plug." You should discuss these important matters with every potential agent or successor agent in advance. You should also request permission from the people you want to name as your agent or successor agent. The person you appoint should not discover that he or she has been appointed via an emergency phone call from some hospital in the middle of the night.

Be very careful in naming a child to make your health care decisions. Many children, even those who have long ago reached the age of majority, have a very difficult time making tough medical decisions for a parent, especially an end-of-life decision. If you want to name children, find out in advance whether they are comfortable with accepting this responsibility and the choices it might entail. If you have more than one child, in what order do you name them? (Remember that some states prohibit joint agents and that appointing joint agents may create conflicts between the individuals appointed.) Do you name them in age order? What if your middle child is a physician or nurse, do you name that child first and then the remaining children in age order? Furthermore, you should recognize that requiring more than one signature for documents related to your treatment might guarantee that the required decisions will not be made in time.

Consider your state's health care statutes for any requirements that they may impose on health care agents. Your attorney can advise you about this, or you can review the statute books at your local library or online. Find a web site (preferably an official state web site) that covers state laws and review your state's policies on living wills, health care agents, or similar subjects.

# ADDITIONAL DECISIONS YOU SHOULD MAKE

There are a host of significant personal decisions you must make to best protect your wishes. These decisions should reflect any nuances of your current and anticipated health status. The paragraphs below provide examples of common issues that affect decisions made by people with chronic illnesses.

### NO HEROIC MEASURES OR ALL MEASURES

Should mechanical means of prolonging your life be used? One difficulty in addressing this question is that it is impossible to know which treatments will be necessary or available. Furthermore, how do you define "heroic"? What is heroic in one situation may not be heroic in another. Since you have COPD, you will assuredly need assistance breathing at some point, and standard forms mandating no intubation may violate your wishes and simply make no sense for you. On the other hand, some forms get quite specific, giving you a complex grid of boxes to check off the types of medical procedures you want or don't want, based on various hypothetical scenarios. But what happens if your scenario is just a little different from what's in the boxes? What should your agent do then? In some cases, having too many choices is worse than having a few. In other cases, not even a form that covers hundreds of options and potential scenarios can get it right—there is simply no guarantee that it will address the unique nuances of your chronic illness or some unanticipated turn of events. Consider different options and provisions and make the choices that are best for you. Review these choices with your health care provider; your doctors and others may help you refine your decisions. If your religion is an important part of your life, you may want to consult with clergy as well.

With so much press and attention given to the right to die, euthanasia, cessation of medical procedures, and related issues, one very important fact has been obscured. Many people want every medically reasonable method, heroic or not, performed, and you may be one of the many. If, for example, there is a breakthrough medical development in the wings that may have a dramatic impact on your chronic illness, you may want every measure taken so that you are still around if and when the breakthrough materializes. You may be more than willing to pursue experimental and new procedures if they can potentially reverse your illness. Most standardized forms don't even address this because they tend to reflect the current broad tendency to prohibit heroic measures. If you do want every life-saving procedure and extraordinary measures (cardiac resuscitation, mechanical respiration, nutrition, hydration) performed, your living will should state this. If you want this only if there is a new potential treatment for your disease, then tailor the language to reflect this.

## NUTRITION AND HYDRATION

You should specifically state whether you would permit your agent to ever withdraw artificial nutrition and hydration. If you do not wish to have artificial feeding, even if discontinuing it could hasten your death, this should be specifically stated. Many states will not permit the cessation of nutrition or hydration unless the patient's living will specifically authorizes it. Because some states require a separate signature (next to the provision) in any health care proxy that permits an agent to withdraw nutrition or hydration, it may be a good idea to sign this provision just to make sure your wishes are not ignored because of a technicality.

Several additional issues can create confusion. How, for example, should "artificial" be defined? Should a distinction be made between withdrawing nutrition and hydration (e.g., a feeding tube) and withholding the initial connection to artificial feeding tubes? Do your religious beliefs affect this decision? The core beliefs of many religions equate the withdrawal, and in some cases the withholding (or nonprovision), of nutrition and hydration as the equivalent of starving someone to death. For this reason, you must consider the religious sensitivities of the people you designate as your health care agents. If someone you want to name as agent would have to violate his or her fundamental religious beliefs to carry out your wishes, deal with this issue now. Depending on your relationship with this individual and your own religious or moral convictions, you may decide to modify your wishes, name a different agent, or get clarification from a religious authority before finalizing your decision.

## QUALITY-OF-LIFE STATEMENTS

Your living will may be the only written evidence of what your deepest personal wishes are. Therefore, it should as clearly and as precisely as possible state your feelings and wishes about health care, treatment, quality of life, whether you may wish to refuse or accept medical treatment, and so forth. The law may require that the living will demonstrate your intent with "clear and convincing evidence." This applies in particularly significant ways to quality-of-life issues. Many living wills contain general language stating that if there is "no quality of life," then "no heroic measures" should be taken to prolong life. But "no quality of life" means different things to different people. For one person, it might mean the inability to communicate to the outside world, with no anticipation of recovery. For someone else, it might mean severe and ongoing pain that cannot be alleviated. Chronic illnesses are, by definition, long-term illnesses, so that you have some understanding of what your future holds. Make specific quality-of-life decisions that work for you. For a young athletic person whose biggest health issue has been a hangnail, the thought of being confined to a wheelchair may appear so traumatic that he or she might in fact define that as "no quality of life" and decline all heroic measures. (Note that such people often change their minds about this when confronted with a major challenge, preferring to fight than succumb without trying.) Someone who has lived with COPD with minimal effect and has recently been told that they have developed additional health problems, may react differently. For you, the definition of quality of life might differ from that presented in either of these examples. It is, in every case, a personal decision that reflects not only physical and mental change but also personal beliefs and numerous other factors that define who you are. Analyze your own feelings and concerns about quality of life and make your wishes explicit.

## GUARDIAN DESIGNATION

If your illness will (or may) result in your eventual inability to manage your affairs and person to the extent that a guardian must be appointed, consider taking the following two steps. First, address all the planning issues and documents presented in this book, especially focusing on a funded revocable living trust. The second step is to include an express provision in your health proxy naming your health proxy as your guardian. Both steps can prevent the need for a court appointed guardian.

There are, generally speaking, two types of guardians. A guardian of your person makes health and living decisions, and a guardian of your property primarily makes financial decisions. Ideally, you should choose who will be making these decisions on your behalf. At a minimum, you should designate your health care agent as both, or at least the guardian of your person. The objective here is to make your wishes known before guardianship becomes an issue. In the event a court in the future has to appoint a guardian, you have made known your wishes about whom that person should be. While there is no guarantee that the court will follow your wishes, significant weight will be given to your designation (especially if your health care proxy is notarized and has two witnesses).

## Sample Provision

"To the extent that I am permitted by law to do so, I hereby nominate my Agent, FINANCIAL AGENT NAME, to serve as the guardian of my property, and my Health Proxy, HEALTH AGENT NAME, to serve as the guardian of my person, or in any similar representative capacity, and if I am not permitted by law to so nominate, then I request that any court that may be involved in the appointment of a guardian, special medical guardian, conservator or similar representative for me give the greatest weight to this request."

### ANATOMICAL GIFTS (ORGAN DONATIONS)

Organ donations help save the lives of others, and it is hoped that you will seriously and carefully give thought to donating your organs after your death. If, however, you do not wish to permit organ donation, you should indicate so in your living will.

Many people erroneously assume that organ donations are prohibited for religious reasons. Often they are not. Do not dismiss organ donations for religious reasons alone unless you have consulted your religious adviser. If the idea of donating your organs to strangers is distasteful to you, consider restricting the provision rather than eliminating it altogether. For example, would you refuse to donate an organ or organs that might save the life of someone you love?

If organ donation is something you believe in and support, you might wish to include an express provision concerning donating tissue samples for research to help others with the same chronic illness you have. The language should be specific enough to ensure that the tissues will be used for research or for whatever specific goal you have in mind. Even if you have a general religious preference against organ donations, you may want to make this an exception. If so, then clearly state that although your stated religious preferences should apply to all other decisions, you have expressly excluded the application of those religious strictures to the donation of tissue for research. You can make a great difference with this simple step.

### Sample Provision

"Because I have lived for many decades with COPD, I expressly include this provision directing the donation of lung tissue samples for COPD research efforts, but for no other purpose. I expressly note and acknowledge that my core religious preferences may mandate against organ donations. Nevertheless, I expressly wish to provide for these tissue donations in spite of any such strictures."

## BURIAL INSTRUCTIONS

If you desire any specific eulogy, service, or steps taken, specify your wishes in your living will. If you want a traditional religious ceremony, say so. If you want to be cremated rather than buried, say so. Alternatively, you can communicate these and other desires in a letter of last instructions.

## RELIGION

Religious preferences, or lack thereof, should be specified. For those with strong religious convictions, it is imperative to specifically address religious concerns to avoid having your beliefs compromised when you may be unable to express your desires. Since health care wishes are such a personal matter, it is also vital to address religious concerns to prevent family members or others involved with your health care from pushing their beliefs (or lack of beliefs) on you. For example, if you are Catholic and wish to have last rites, your living will should so state.

The legal community, right-to-die organizations, and many others involved with the health care decision process have too often ignored religious considerations assuming that most people signing living wills while they are healthy aren't concerned about religious issues. These organizations, however, fail to comprehend that many of these same people, when faced with a major catastrophe such as serious illness or loss of a close family member, fall back on their religious roots for guidance and comfort. Unfortunately, in the case of chronic illnesses that eventually lead to cognitive impairment, it may then be too late for these people or their loved ones to express spiritual changes. The solution is to think about this issue and the religious implications of the entire health care process while you are able to. In the end, there will be no regrets that something important was not addressed. (For more detail on religion and its potential impact on estate planning, see Chapter 12.)

Whether or not you have any religious convictions, your living will should communicate your decisions. If you were born to parents with a particular religious affiliation, other members of your family could assume that it would be appropriate to consult with clergy of your religious background before making a decision. This may or may not be what you wish to have done. Religiously influenced decisions can well be different from what you want. For example, several religions restrict the ability to stop heroic measures. If you want nutrition and hydration withdrawn if there is no hope of your regaining quality of life, it is important to communicate whether you wish religious principles to be considered in making this decision.

Religious doctrines may have a very specific effect on what can be done medically to sustain or not sustain life. However you presently feel about the effects the tenets of your faith may have on these decisions, it can be a terrible mistake not to address these issues with your clergy. Your family's religious convictions should also be considered. With some modification, it may be possible to carry out your wishes in a manner that does not negate the religious tenets of your faith.

If you decide, after consulting with your clergy, and discussions with your family, that you wish to take a position contrary to the tenets of your faith (e.g., for tissue donations as discussed above), your living will should indicate this in very precise terms. You may wish to provide the name and address of a clergy member to your attorney so that the clergy member can be consulted for interpretations of your religious beliefs. You should include in a note of instruction, and in some instances even in your legal documents, the name of the religious adviser to be contacted if a decision has to be made concerning your care and the decision cannot be easily made without religious interpretation. Also, you should include the name and contact data for the religious organization or institution to be contacted should the clergy member you named be unavailable. It is quite important that you discuss these matters with your personal religious adviser before you meet with your lawyer.

### PAIN RELIEF

What about pain medication and other treatments or procedures to reduce pain? Should they be administered even if they hasten death? Is there any adverse religious implications if pain relief hastens death? Should a distinction be made between the side effects of pain relief somewhat hastening death and affirmatively using pain medication in doses intended to cause death? How can this distinction be made? Are there any specific implications of your illness that may effect how you want to mandate pain relief? Your answers to these and similar questions should become part of your living will.

## WILL AMBULANCE AND EMERGENCY MEDICAL TECHNICIANS ACCEPT A LIVING WILL?

The primary goal of ambulance and emergency medical technicians is saving lives, or more specifically, keeping a patient alive until he or she reaches a hospital. The urgent nature of their activities, the time frame of their involvement, and their primary mission make it difficult if not impossible for them to review, interpret, and then apply the provisions of your living will. Plan in advance.

If you are at a stage at which you would not want heroic measures, you may prefer to consider alternative transportation arrangements to the hospital to avoid having the emergency personnel performing heroic measures in the ambulance. Discuss this with your health care agents and doctor in advance.

## WHAT ABOUT OLD LIVING WILLS?

It is best to locate and destroy old living wills. This is especially wise if your prior living will and health proxy were signed prior to your diagnosis. Being diagnosed with a COPD changes almost everything about these documents, including how you view any future health care issues. Most likely, your wishes and needs will have evolved significantly and the modifications will be reflected in your new living will. The danger of keeping old living wills is that they may inadvertently surface at the wrong time in the wrong place (or in the wrong hands) and cause unnecessary confusion. To preclude such an event, make sure the appropriate people have the newest living will you have signed. You might also consider including a provision revoking any and all prior living wills. However, it is still best to locate and destroy these prior documents.

# What To Do with Your Signed Living Will Forms

Give a copy of your living will and health care proxy to your primary care doctor. Give your initial agent, and at least one successor agent, an original. Most importantly, keep an original at home in an accessible location.

# Other Steps You Should Take

### DISCUSS YOUR DECISIONS

The process by which you determine what your living will should contain is just as important as the documents you sign. This process should therefore include candid discussions about your feelings with your family, loved ones, doctor, and religious adviser (if applicable). All of these people may be involved in the decisions concerning your health care if you should become unable to express your own wishes. They cannot be expected to carry out your desires without knowing what those desires are and how you feel about them. The more openly you discuss your feelings with family, friends, and loved ones, the more likely that you can ease the burden of the decision making they face. While your religious adviser can assist your doctors and family in reaching a decision that is in accordance with applicable religious tenets and your personal beliefs, an awareness of your feelings can be important in properly guiding your family and physicians. The process of communicating your beliefs and feelings is very important; it cannot be accomplished by signing a quick-fix form with your lawyer.

### COORDINATE YOUR HEALTH CARE AND FINANCIAL DOCUMENTS

A durable power of attorney with financial powers is an integral part of your health care (and estate) planning. If the agent you authorize does not have the financial wherewithal, or the legal access to your funds to carry out your health care wishes, then your desires could also be stymied. Financial considerations should be addressed as a separate document since some states do not permit the granting of health care and financial powers in the same document. This can be particularly important if your attitude about the religious implications of a living will or health care proxy differs from that of family members. As an alternative, a living trust (not to be confused with a living will), which is also called a revocable inter vivos trust, can be used. When properly prepared, this document can address a broad range of financial and other issues, including the handling of your financial matters in the event of disability, much more comprehensively than a power of attorney. The living trust remains a powerful and flexible financial planning tool for handling your financial matters in the event of disability. To make your power of attorney or living trust effective, be certain that your attorney-in-fact or trustees have adequate financial information to locate and marshal your assets for your benefit. The best legal documents are useless if family members can't locate your bank or securities accounts to apply your assets to meet your health care wishes.

## CARRY A POCKET CARD

Whatever your wishes concerning your health care, properly prepared documents are far too bulky to carry on your person. In an emergency situation, your attending physicians can at least be informed by a wallet card that you signed a living will and health care proxy, and whom to contact. It might also specify the major health issues you face. This is especially important if you don't wear a medical identification bracelet or other identifying device.

## CONSIDER THE POLICIES OF A PARTICULAR HEALTH CARE FACILITY

If you are going to enter a nursing home or other health care facility, be certain to review its policies about fundamental health care issues. If the organization's policies are incompatible with your health care wishes, you may wish to evaluate alternative facilities. For example, if the facility is sponsored by a Catholic organization, there may be a strict policy against assisted suicide or euthanasia. This policy may not be effected no matter what is stated in your living will. A Jewish health care facility may have a policy of administering nutrition and hydration unless medically contraindicated. If you are a Jehovah's Witness, identify medical institutions familiar with and able to address your special religious/medical needs. In some cases, if you have chosen a particular course of action in your living will, you may need to select the medical facility with similar policies about care and advance planning.

## CHAPTER SUMMARY

This chapter has reviewed two key health care decision documents: your living will and health care proxy. These documents are important to your dignity as a human being, to minimize emotional stress on your loved ones, and to ensure that your wishes are respected. This means taking the time and effort to craft these documents to address COPD and any other current known health conditions, the likely issues that may arise in the future as a result of your chronic illness, and any religious convictions you have.

**Caution:** The living will document on the following pages is merely an illustration and you must discuss the appropriate form to use with an attorney in your state.

# LIVING WILL

I, *YOUR NAME, residing at *YOUR ADDRESS, being an adult and of sound mind, and being competent and otherwise capable of making the decisions set forth in this Living Will, and having the fundamental right to make voluntary, informed choices to accept, reject, or choose among alternative courses of medical and surgical treatment, make this declaration as a directive to be followed if for any reason I become unable to participate in decisions regarding my medical care, this statement shall stand as an expression of my wishes, beliefs, objectives and directions (my "Wishes"). It is my specific intent that my Wishes, as stated herein constitute clear and convincing evidence of such Wishes.

**Recitals.**

**a. WHEREFORE**, I direct that this Living Will become a part of my permanent medical records. I expressly authorize any medical care provider to rely on the statements in this Living Will if it is not feasible in an emergency situation to reach my Health Care Agent. This Living Will shall serve as general guidance for my Agent appointed under my separate Health Care Proxy or Health Care Power of Attorney. However, in all circumstances, medical care providers may defer to the judgment and interpretation of my Health Care Agent of the terms of this Living Will and shall in no event be held liable for relying on my Health Care Agent's interpretations. I expressly recognize that it is impossible to conceive of all situations that may occur in a living will so that my Agent may address all such circumstances using the guidelines contained in this Living Will.

**b. WHEREFORE**, I wish to direct the actions of my family, friends, physicians, nurses, and all those concerned with my care, as provided in this declaration.

**c. WHEREFORE**, I hereby express my hope that my Wishes be honored by health care facilities and physicians without having to go through the process of any judicial or other determination.

**NOW THEREFORE**, I declare my wishes to be as follows:

## 1. Current, Known, or Suspected Medical Conditions.

a. I am presently living with [Chronic bronchitis] [Refractory asthma] [Emphysema] [Bronchiectasis]
**Comment**: *Describe any details of COPD relevant and how it may impact decision making.*

**b. Comment**: *Describe any other comorbid/current medical conditions and how it may impact medical decision making.*

## 2. No Heroic Medical Efforts.

a. General 'No Heroic Measures' Language.

(1) **Comment: Chronic Illness:** *You may want every medically reasonable method, heroic or not, performed, intubation is but one example of a step you might want performed unless your situation has worsened to "terminal" which you might define as less than three months to live even if intubated.. If there is a breakthrough medical development in the wings that may have a dramatic impact on your chronic illness, you may want every measure taken. You may be more than willing to pursue experimental and new procedures if they could potentially reverse your illness. Most standardized forms not only don't contemplate this, but would likely result in treating these as prohibited "heroic measures." If you want every life-saving procedure and extraordinary measures (cardiac resuscitation, mechanical respiration, nutrition, hydration) performed, your living will should state this. If you only want this if there is a new potential treatment for your disease, then tailor the language to reflect this.*

(2) **Sample COPD Provision to Modify:** "I have COPD which is presently incurable and irreversible and which will result in continued difficulties breathing. If I reach a stage of profound dementia, or am terminal (defined as more likely than not unable to survive for three months regardless of the procedures taken) and I have a nearly complete or a complete lack of awareness of my surroundings, I wish that no heroic measures be taken to preserve my life, and for this purpose, and only at this medical condition, intubation shall be deemed heroic."

(3) *General No Heroic Measures Language. If:*

(a) I have an incurable or irreversible, severe mental or severe physical condition; or am in a state of permanent unconsciousness or profound dementia; or am severely injured, or have a terminal illness (for purposes of the above, "terminal illness" shall be defined as an irreversible, incurable, and untreatable condition caused by disease, illness, or injury when an attending physician can certify in writing that, to a reasonable degree of medical certainty, there is no hope of my recovery or death is likely to occur in a brief period of time if life-sustaining treatment is not provided. "Permanently unconscious" is defined as a state that, to a reasonable degree of medical certainty, an attending physician certifies in writing that I am irreversibly unaware of myself and my environment and there is a total loss of cerebral cortical functioning resulting in my having no capacity to experience pain); and

(b) In any of these cases there is no reasonable expectation of recovering from such severe, permanent condition, and regaining any meaningful quality of life, then in any such event, it is my desire and intent that heroic life-sustaining procedures and extraordinary maintenance or medical treatment be withheld and withdrawn.

(c) Quality of life is of tremendous importance in determining the scope and extent of health care services which I wish to receive. Maintaining my life as a mere biological existence, in a vegetative state, is not an acceptable goal of my medical treatment. Therefore, if there is no reasonable probability (i.e., negligible probability) that any particular medical treatment would benefit me by returning me to a level of functioning or existence where I could communicate with my loved ones, and reasonably understand such communication, I direct that medical treatments, as described herein, be withheld and withdrawn.

(1) **Comment:** *Should the "quality of life" provisions be modified*

(d) It is not my desire to prolong my life through mechanical means where my body is no longer able to perform vital bodily functions on its own, and where there is little likelihood of ever regaining any meaningful quality of life. The condition and degree of severity and permanence contemplated by this provision are of such a nature and degree of permanent illness, injury, disability, or accompanied by pain such that the average person would make the decisions I have made herein.

(e) In any such event, I direct all physicians and medical facilities in whose care I may be, and my family and all those concerned with my care, to refrain from and cease extraordinary or heroic life sustaining treatment to be withheld and withdrawn (i.e., to be considered heroic) include, without limitation, surgery, antibiotics, cardiac and pulmonary resuscitation, ventilation, intubation, or other respiratory support (except as provided hereinabove or as provided under the provision below "Nutrition and Hydration"), medical and surgical tests and treatments and medications diagnostic tests of any nature, and surgical procedures of any nature.

**3. Nutrition and Hydration.** If any attending physician shall state in writing that I am, to a reasonable degree of medical certainty, in a terminal condition or a permanently unconscious state, and that the provision (or continued provision) of nutrition and hydration will not, to a reasonable degree of medical certainty, prolong my life in accordance with my wishes, provide comfort to me, or minimize my pain or discomfort, then I authorize and direct that the provision of further nutrition or hydration may cease.

I AGREE TO ABOVE NUTRITION/HYDRATION PROVISION:

_____

*YOUR NAME

**4. Medication and Treatments to Alleviate Pain and Suffering.**

a. Even if procedures and treatments are to be withheld or withdrawn, I wish that all palliative treatment and measures for my comfort, and to alleviate my pain, be continued.

b. Such efforts to relieve pain may be continued even if such measures may: shorten my life, lead to permanent addiction, have potentially dangerous ancillary consequences, render me unconscious, or lead to permanent physical damage.

**5. Wishes Concerning Living Arrangements.**

a. *Comment: Elaborate and provide detail, discuss hospice care arrangements.*

b. It is my wish that I live in my home rather than a institution, hospital, nursing home, or other facility, if such an arrangement would not jeopardize the chance of a meaningful recovery, impose undue burden on my family, or prevent my obtaining maximum pain relief for any illness from which I suffer.

c. Although I have some preference to reside in my home with care, if no family member is living with me, and only hired help can be obtained, I request that my Agent, in my Agent's discretion, weigh the benefits of such an environment to that of a better health care facility, if available. By way of example and not limitation, the services and socialization of a health care facility should be considered.

**6. Transfer or Removal to Another Health Care Facility.**

a. In the event that any health care facility in which I am located is unwilling or unable to carry out my Wishes, I authorize my being moved to another health care facility, even one located in a different state (and to facilitate such a removal I expressly authorize that the laws of such other state may be designated to govern this document). I direct that my health care providers cooperate with, and assist in, promptly transferring me to another health care facility if necessary for my care or to carry out my Wishes.

b. I further direct my medical care provider to transfer a copy of all of my medical records with me in such instance. This authorization to release medical records, to any health care facility to which I am transferred, is expressly intended to constitute a full authorization and release under HIPAA of any such information, including but not limited to private health information. I specifically indemnify and hold harmless any medical care facility releasing me and my records for such purpose.

**7. Careful Consideration Has Been Made of Decisions in This Document.**

a. These decisions and requests are made after careful consideration and reflection.

b. These decisions are made to avoid the indignity, pain and difficulties, both for myself and my family, of prolonged, hopeless deterioration and dependence where I am in a condition described above.

**8. Religious Convictions: General Statement.**

a. *Option 1: No Religious Restrictions Should Apply.* I do not wish to condition the effectiveness of this directive upon its conforming to any *RELIGION or other religious doctrines or beliefs to which I may be believed to subscribe.

b. *Option 2: Religious Principles Shall Apply to the Interpretation of This Living Will.* I wish to condition the effectiveness of this directive upon its conforming to *RELIGION doctrines and beliefs to which I subscribe. In order to effectuate my Wishes, if any question arises as to the requirements of my religious beliefs, I direct that the guidance of a religious advisor selected in accordance with my statement of religious beliefs made in this paragraph be sought.

**9. Organ Donation. Comment:** *If you have a chronic or other Illness you may wish to provide for a specific donation of lung tissue to permit research to combat COPD.* Because I have lived for many decades with COPD I expressly include this provision directing the donation of lung tissue samples for COPD research efforts, but for no other purpose. I expressly note and acknowledge that my core religious preferences may mandate against organ donations, nevertheless, I expressly wish to provide for these tissue donations in spite of any such strictures.

**10. Funeral and Related Arrangements.**

**a. Comment:** *Select, modify, or provide guidance as to funeral and other last arrangements. Consider the provisions as possible suggestions.*

b. *Religious Principles Shall Apply to Funeral and Other Arrangements.* Notwithstanding any statements above concerning inapplicability of religious doctrines, I specifically request that:

(1) My funeral service and arrangements and burial be in accordance with *RELIGION religious customs.

(2) A burial plot and marker may be purchased in accordance with my wishes, and to make such other arrangements as are appropriate, if I have not already done so myself.

(3) Cremation, and internment of my remains, including the purchase of a place of internment.

**11. No Time Limit; Duration.** I have considered the possibility of limiting the effectiveness of this instrument to a fixed period of time from the date hereof and have decided that it shall remain in full force and effect for as long as I may live. This Living Will may be so relied upon by any person or institution unless such person or institution has actually received a written notice of revocation or change.

**12. Morally Binding.** These directions are the exercise of my right to refuse treatment. Therefore, I expect my family, physicians, and all those concerned with my care to regard themselves as legally (whether of not required by the law at the time of the execution, or the place of implementation, of this Living Will) and morally bound to act in accordance with these directions. In doing so they will be free from any liability and responsibility for having followed my Wishes.

**13. Revocation of Prior Grants.** This document revokes any prior living will, executed by me.

**14. Copies of Document.** A copy, facsimile, PDF, or other electronic transmission or copy of an executed version of this document shall be as valid as the original. I ask that a copy of this document be made part of my permanent medical record.

**15. Competency to Execute Documents.** I understand the full import of this document and I am emotionally and mentally competent to execute it.

**16. Construction and Interpretation of This Document.**

a. The provisions of this entire document are separable so that the invalidity of one or more provisions shall not affect any others.

b. Should legislation or regulations be enacted after the execution of this Living Will, then this Living Will shall, to the extent necessary to make it valid and enforceable, be interpreted so as to comply with such future legislation or regulations in the manner which most closely approximates my Wishes.

c. Any titles and captions contained in this article are for convenience only and should not be read to affect the meaning of any provision.

IN WITNESS WHEREOF, I have executed this declaration *MONTH *DAY, *YEAR.

_____

*YOUR NAME

Witness: _____

State of *STATE-EXECUTION

County of *COUNTY NAME)

On this *MONTH *DAY, *YEAR, before me, the subscriber, a notary of the State of *STATE-EXECUTION, personally appeared *YOUR NAME who, I am satisfied after inspection of *STATENAME driver's license, is the principal mentioned in, and who signed the Living Will and acknowledged that he or she signed, sealed and delivered the same as his or her act and deed, that he or she appeared to be of sound mind and not under any duress, fraud or undue influence, and for the uses and purposes therein expressed.

_____

Notary Signature

DECLARATION OF WITNESSES TO LIVING WILL FOR MEDICAL DECISIONS

The undersigned each hereby declare and attest that: (1) the Living Will was personally signed, sealed, and delivered by *YOURNAME, in my presence, and I, at *YOUR NAME's request and in *YOUR NAME's presence and in the presence of the other witnesses, I subscribed my name as a witness; (2) I did not sign the signature of *YOUR NAME; (3) I am acquainted with *YOUR NAME and believe *YOUR NAME to be of sound mind and under no constraint, duress or undue influence; (4) I am not related to *YOUR NAME by blood or marriage; (5) I am not, to the best of my knowledge, entitled to any portion of the estate of *YOUR NAME under any Will of *YOUR NAME or Codicil now existing, nor am I so entitled by operation of law; (6) I do not have any present or inchoate claim against any portion of *YOUR NAME's estate or for *YOUR NAME's medical care; (7) I am not a physician attending to *YOUR NAME as a patient; and (8) I am over eighteen (18) years of age.

| Printed Name of Witness | Address (City and State) of Witness | Signature of Witness |
|---|---|---|
|  |  |  |
|  |  |  |

## CHAPTER 9

# Your Will

## Distributing Assets and Caring for Your Loved Ones

## Why Your Will Is Not the Focus of This Book

ASK ALMOST ANYONE ABOUT ESTATE PLANNING and the first, and often only, step mentioned is preparing a will. So why is your will, if it is so important, not the focus of this book? The answer is simple. The focus of this book is on planning for those with COPD and their loved ones to address and custom tailor estate planning in a sensitive and rational manner. While your will is an essential part of your estate plan, and possibly the key document governing the distribution of your assets on death, and the appointment of a guardian if you have minor children, it is not much different from wills executed by people who do not have to contend with COPD. Because the format (and use) of wills is generally the same for you as it is for other people, this chapter will be shorter and simpler than others in this book. You can generally rely on other general publications that deal with the issue of wills in greater detail. Bear in mind that a living trust may serve you better as your key document.

A few points should be considered as to the differences you, as result of your chronic illness, may face with respect to your will:

❖ Planning to manage your assets for the duration of your life, especially if you are likely to experience cognitive impairment, will likely increase the importance of your planning of other documents that will be important to safeguard your financial interests while you are alive. This is because the manner in which you own (title) assets may be modified to facilitate management of your affairs. A funded revocable living trust will make your will less important to the disposition of your assets upon your death, but it does not negate the need for a will (see Chapter 10).

❖    You should consider making a bequest to charitable organizations dedicated to serving those living with COPD to provide services to those living with COPD or perhaps to fund research to find additional treatment options. If you have the financial wherewithal to provide charitable support to a charity or foundation that has helped you, you are encouraged to help others.

❖    Although your will may not have any unusual provisions, if your family or loved ones draft wills, their wills may need to be modified to include a special needs trust for you, if that is warranted. This is a trust that can benefit you but not cause you to lose government benefits.

## WHAT IS A WILL?

A will, or Last Will and Testament, is a document in which you (the testator) state how your money and assets are to be distributed upon your death. Your will can also appoint an executor, who is a person that is responsible for managing your estate. Through your will, you appoint guardians to care for any minor children you may have. You can also name trustees to handle any trusts you may have set up in your will (a testamentary trust).

Everyone needs a will, and you are no exception. Even if you own assets jointly or fund a living trust, there is no assurance that some assets will not be governed by those arrangements. Your will may determine how your money is distributed on your death, but it can also accomplish much more. A properly prepared and executed will can protect your loved ones and ensure that your wishes are carried out.

## ASSETS NOT AFFECTED BY YOUR WILLS

Many assets you own will not be distributed under your will. These may include:

❖    IRA and other retirement plans, which have beneficiary designation forms that govern the passing of those assets to the people you name.

❖    Life insurance policies, which are typically paid to the persons you name in the policy application (or a beneficiary change form you sign later), not by your will.

❖ Jointly owned assets, such as a bank account that reads "John Smith and Jane Doe, as joint tenants with rights of survivorship," which pass to Jane on John's death without regard to a will.

❖ Some bank and other accounts can be owned in a manner that transfers ownership on death outside of your will, such as a "pay on death" or "in trust for" account. For example, "John Smith, in trust for Jane Doe" or "John Smith, pay on death to, Jane Doe" will pass to Jane automatically on John's death.

❖ If you use a revocable living trust to protect you, assets held by that trust will not pass under your will, but rather as directed by the trust document.

The fact that many, most, or even all, of your assets pass outside of your will reflects the danger you face if you buy a cheap will from a website. Such sites will not address the overall planning and relevance of your will in the context of your assets, goals, and so on. What you really need is an estate planning specialist who is experienced in dealing with such matters. A professionally prepared will assuredly cost more than an online will, but that cost may well be justified by avoiding significant problems if title to your assets, beneficiary designations, and your will are not coordinated.

## What to Include in Your Will

Your will should include the standard basic information most wills include: who your assets will be distributed to (spouse, partner, children, or friends) and the manner you want them distributed (outright transfer, trusts, at specific ages, etc.). You can also use your will to appoint a guardian for your minor children. You will name the executor of your will who will manage the winding up of your personal financial matters, collect your assets, pay final bills and taxes, and distribute the remaining assets to your heirs. You can also name the trustees who will be handling the financial aspects of any trusts set up to manage assets for your heirs.

## CHAPTER SUMMARY

This chapter has provided a brief overview of what your will is, some of the items to include in your will, and the few ways your will be might differ from those who are not living with a chronic illness. You should take advantage of the many available books and resources that focus on wills and living trusts to learn more; generally, will planning applicable to the public at large also applies to you.

## CHAPTER 10

# REVOCABLE LIVING TRUST
## MAINTAINING CONTROL AND PROTECTING YOU THROUGH DISABILITY

## A REVOCABLE LIVING TRUST: THE MOST IMPORTANT DOCUMENT YOU MAY EVER SIGN

A REVOCABLE LIVING TRUST (sometimes called a "living trust," "loving trust," or "revocable inter vivos trust") might be the most powerful and beneficial tool to assist you in managing assets and other matters throughout the often unpredictable course of COPD and any other health challenges you might have. Careful attention, however, has to be given to this type of planning, and especially in your use of other materials made available to the public on living trusts. The reason for this is that almost all materials on living trusts focus on avoiding probate (the process of administering your will and assets following death). Not to negate the benefits some feel that probate avoidance might provide, this is not the primary benefit for most people living with COPD. Let's focus on "living" and the good this technique can provide to you.

As explained in Chapter 9, the manner in which you dispose of assets on death is really not different from the manner used by anyone else. Avoiding probate is rarely the big deal most books and "authorities" make it sound, but regardless, it is not an issue unique to you. Your living trust, on the other hand, should be a document planned and tailored to provide careful management of your assets during your life. This is especially important if your COPD or other illnesses, if any, progress in a manner that diminishes and perhaps eliminates your ability to manage your own financial and legal affairs. The type of living trust you need has a very different focus from the ones typically used and sold to the general public. This chapter will explain the technique and document, but will limit its focus to the matters most important to you. Therefore, you will need to supplement the information provided here with materials of a more general nature.

### SOME REVOCABLE LIVING TRUST JARGON

A basic review of some of the legal jargon used in connection with a revocable living trust will make it easier for you to understand the discussions that follow:

❖     A living trust is a trust that you set up during your lifetime. In legal jargon, a "living" trust is often referred to as an "inter vivos" trust.

❖     In legal jargon, you are called the "trustor," "grantor," or "settler."

❖     A "trust" is a legal contract, made between you and the trustees, to accomplish the purposes stated in the document (called the "trust" or the "trust indenture").

❖     The "trustees" are the persons charged with managing the trust assets (called "corpus") for the purposes stated in the trust document. The trustees are "fiduciaries," people occupying a position of trust and held to a high standard of care and responsibility under the law.

❖     The trustees manage the trust assets for the people the trust document lists as benefiting from the trust. These people are referred to as "beneficiaries."

❖     Living trusts are almost always written to be "revocable." This means that you can change your living trust at any time. This standard definition, however, leaves out a vital concept for you in light of your chronic illness. If your competency wanes to a point where you no longer have "contractual capacity" (a higher standard than mere testamentary capacity to sign a will), you will no longer be able to change your trust document. It will then become irrevocable. So, while your living trust may be revocable for a time, it may become irrevocable well before your death. But should that occur, you will have likely been wise to have put in place the trust to protect your interests.

## WHAT IS A REVOCABLE LIVING TRUST?

As noted above, a living trust is a trust that you set up during your lifetime. You retain complete control over the assets in the trust while you are alive and competent. If you become unable to manage the trust, because of disability, hospitalization, or other issues, an alternate or "successor" trustee takes over managing your trust assets. This is an important point that warrants emphasis. The trustee of your living trust has no control over any assets not specifically included in your trust. So if you will be relying on your trust for protection, you need to transfer the assets to your trust for it to afford this protection to your trust (called "funding"). This might entail no more than having your broker change the name on your brokerage account from "John Smith" to the "John Smith and Sandra Jones, co-trustees of the John Smith Revocable Living Trust dated June 12, 2011."

The trustees of your trust are permitted to act only for the benefit of the beneficiaries of the trust, typically and primarily you, in accordance with the terms of the trust agreement. Although you may be the primary beneficiary, you don't have to be the only beneficiary. You can name other loved ones as beneficiaries too. Even if funds in the trust can only be used for your care during your lifetime, they will be distributed to your named heirs following your death. Most revocable trusts are drafted with the grantor of the trust (you) as the sole trustee. Because of COPD, however, it might be better for you to name a cotrustee at the inception (creation) of the trust. If and when you are no longer capable of handling your own affairs, your co-trustee will be able to act on your behalf with a wide range of powers, solely with the purpose of benefiting you. Naming a co-trustee prevents time-consuming and convoluted impediments to carrying out your wishes and ensures that someone has the legal right to access and manage your assets to best provide for you. If you suffer an exacerbation, or are hospitalized for several weeks, having another person named as co-trustee and a trust agreement that authorizes either co-trustee to alone handle ministerial and administrative tasks (like paying routine bills) can provide a great safety net for you as well as peace of mind that your affairs will be handled in the event of an emergency.

For income tax purposes, the trust is generally ignored and all income and deductions are reported on your own tax return. Because there is no current tax benefit of setting up a living trust, the format used can be quite flexible so it is adaptable to meet a broad range of your personal objectives.

On your death, provisions that serve the same purpose as a will apply to govern the disposition of your assets.

## OTHER REASONS WHY YOU SHOULD HAVE A REVOCABLE LIVING TRUST

A revocable living trust may be the ideal vehicle for someone living with COPD. It allows for the most comprehensive, detailed planning for any disability. In the appropriate circumstances, living trusts can be an ideal vehicle to serve your needs throughout the course of your disease. If it is possible that you may periodically, or at some date entirely, require assistance and support with your financial affairs, this type of planning should be evaluated. If you have a disease course punctuated by frequent exacerbations, you may need someone to step in and assist you on a sporadic basis. In this event, having a revocable living trust and a successor and co-trustees can be ideal. This arrangement enables your co-trustee to act immediately, and to use your funds for your benefit. While your agent under your power of attorney can also do this, having a co-trustee of a revocable living trust allows all necessary actions to occur more quickly, easily, and effectively. A bank or other institution will more readily accept the signature of a co-trustee than that of an agent acting in your name. This is because the title (legal ownership) of the assets are in the trustee's name as trustee. In the case of an agent under a power of attorney, the assets remain in your name and the agent has to act upon them. Having both can facilitate carrying out your important personal objectives and offers you the best protection.

A living trust may also be a good idea for someone who does not have an adequate safety net of relatives or close friends to rely upon. With a living trust, you can name a bank or trust company as sole or co-trustee. The benefit to this is that a bank or trust company brings integrity, independence, and professionalism to the management of your trust and affairs. An institution won't serve as agent under your power of attorney.

## WHO SHOULD NOT HAVE A REVOCABLE LIVING TRUST

A revocable living trust is not for everyone. If you cannot afford the cost of an attorney who specializes in estate planning to draft the trust, it may not be worthwhile to pursue this option. If you do not have significant assets to transfer to your revocable living trust, there is probably no need to create a trust of this kind. You might be quite wealthy, but if your assets are primarily in retirement accounts and life insurance policies, there may be few if any assets you probably would want to transfer to a revocable living trust (although planning with other types of trusts to maximize tax or asset protection goals may still be warranted).

## HOW COPD AFFECTS YOUR REVOCABLE LIVING TRUST

As was explained in Chapter 4 of this book, the level of competency required to sign a trust, which is legally a contract, is higher than the level of competency required to sign a will. Because of the higher level of competency required, it is advisable to establish your trust early on, so that any possible cognitive symptoms COPD might conceivably cause cannot be used to challenge the trust. The trust can be challenged on the basis of undue influence, mental incompetence, or lack of advice from independent counsel. Mental incompetence can be established from the testimony of physicians and others who provide treatment, although ultimately it is a legal determination. Creating and signing the trust too late may make its validity questionable.

Revocable trusts are an ideal technique to assist many people living with a chronic illness to manage assets. However, as with the durable power of attorney discussed in Chapter 5, there are special nuances for you to consider. The typical revocable trust is drafted with the grantor as sole trustee. But if you have severe COPD, or complications from other health challenges, it may be best if you are named a co-trustee. But in contrast to many other chronic illnesses, unless you have had a significant cognitive impact you will probably choose to serve at least as a co-trustee. If you are the sole trustee and experience an exacerbation (something that typically occurs with COPD), it might prove problematic. Not naming yourself as trustee at all, however, cedes control from you even though you will generally have the capacity to make decisions. Relying on a transition to a successor trustee not only creates the expected issues with triggering the transition (as with a springing power of attorney), but also results in your complete removal as trustee, which may be unwarranted.

Most people with COPD would be expected to resume their involvement as trustee when an exacerbation subsides. Thus, having another person serve along with you as co-trustees from inception is probably a wise choice. In addition, the trust document could state that either trustee alone should have the authority to act independently to take the actions that might be required during periods of an exacerbation or flare-up. This might include signature authority over banking matters, but might expressly exclude the right to sign an income tax return (but permit filing an extension or paying tax) or to sell an asset over some specified value. Significant decisions can be deferred until the exacerbation ends or expressly reserved to your discretion unless there is a permanent disability. The use of a co-trustee and these modifications to the typical trust language can provide an ideal solution for you and can give you maximum control while simultaneously creating a mechanism that ensures continuity during an unexpected attack.

## Sample Provision

"Any trustee, acting alone and without any requirement for joint action, is authorized and permitted to make ministerial and administrative decisions, including, but not limited to, routine banking, investment, and brokerage transactions."

## REVOCABLE LIVING TRUST HYPE AND FACT

A revocable trust is one of the most talked about estate planning techniques, but much of the talk is hype. Living trusts in the appropriate circumstances can be an ideal tool to accomplish many essential planning goals. In inappropriate circumstances, they can be an unnecessary waste of time and money, and create some unnecessary hassles and complications in managing your affairs. In a worst-case scenario you may use (or be sold) a revocable living trust when another technique would have been more appropriate. The results could be disastrous, especially if the planning ignores protecting you throughout the course of your chronic illness. Understanding how to look through the puffery will help you make better decisions:

❖   *Hype*: A living trust will solve all your problems.

❖   *Fact*: Slick sales pitches and canned documents will not address your specific needs. You need a document tailored to your personal situation, prepared by an attorney that specializes in estate planning. All the other planning discussed in this book—budget, financial plan, power of attorney, health proxy, and so on—are all tailored to reflect COPD.

### EXAMPLE

Living trusts are often promoted at slick sales seminars, in some cases not even presented by attorneys specializing in estate planning. After the scare tactics and donuts, you'll often be pressured to sign up for a "free" consultation. If you sign up for the living trust after the consultation, too often you'll wind up with prepackaged documents. Many of these marketing programs are often tied to independent companies that produce canned documents based on a generic questionnaire. The key problem for you with this approach is that the living trust documents you get will be very generic. This could be especially problematic if your situation is handled by an attorney who is not an estate planning specialist. While these plans and documents might be useful to avoiding probate, they may not address any of the specific COPD issues in this book, and they may not be tailored at all to issues of managing your life as your COPD progresses. These companies may refuse (or lack the capability) to tailor the trust documents to the unique issues of your illness.

❖     *Hype*: A living trust avoids probate, the key problem.

❖     *Fact*: Living trusts, even when completed effectively with full consideration to your health concerns, will not solve all of your planning problems.

EXAMPLE

Assume you live in Vermont and have a rental vacation property in Pennsylvania. A living trust will avoid probate for the Pennsylvania property. (Avoiding probate is one of the purported great benefits of a living trust.) A living trust, however, will not facilitate making gifts of interests in that property to reduce your estate tax cost. A limited liability company ("LLC") can achieve these two goals. Using a living trust instead of an LLC would be less than ideal. But it gets worse. If you use a living trust to avoid ancillary probate and are sued for more than your insurance coverage by an injured tenant (or your policy has an exception for the incident involved), your entire estate could be jeopardized. If, instead, you transferred the property to an LLC, you would limit your liability only to the property in question. Your home and other assets would be safe. Assuming the living trust covers all contingencies can be disastrous. While living trusts can be incredibly helpful, they are only one step in a comprehensive plan.

❖     *Hype*: A living trust is necessary to avoid probate.

❖     *Fact*: Many people have the majority or even all of their assets pass outside of the probate process without a trust. Also, in most situations probate is really not that big a deal.

A living trust is primarily touted for its use as a method of avoiding probate. Probate, although it can be expensive in certain cases, is not necessarily the evil and excessively expensive process many people fear. Moreover, there are simple and no-cost ways to avoid probate when avoiding probate is appropriate. For example, naming your intended heirs as beneficiaries and not your estate avoids probate for insurance and retirement plans and other assets. The appropriate ownership (title) of assets, as explained above, can also make probate unnecessary.

❖    *Hype*: Living trusts are simple, inexpensive, and easy.

❖    *Fact*: A living trust, especially when tailored to address the circumstances of your chronic illness, your needs, your objectives, and so forth, may not be simple or inexpensive. It may be quite worthwhile, but it may require more effort and cost to set up with the level of detailed planning you might need.

A living trust is not necessarily the simple and inexpensive document many people expect (unless you use a cookie-cutter version like the one described earlier in this chapter). To properly set up a living trust, you must retain a lawyer to properly prepare a comprehensive plan and, based on that plan, a trust document. The trust document, if properly prepared, is not as simple as most sales pitches would have you believe. It is tailored to address your personal goals and objectives, estate tax (if any), and other needs. Be certain that the attorney you retain coordinates the tax allocation clause in your will with the tax clause in the trust. The trust document, however, is only step one. You should generally arrange to transfer many of your assets to the trust. For real estate, you will need to execute a deed and, depending on where you live, complete various tax and other forms. If the property has a mortgage, you will have to review the mortgage for a due-on-sale clause and most likely notify your bank. Insurance policies on real estate and art will have to be changed to the name of the trust to be effective. The title insurance company that insured any real estate you want to transfer to the living trust should be asked whether a new policy in the name of the trust is required. Personal property will require a bill of sale to effect transfer. Bank accounts should often be retitled into the name of your trust, and it might be advisable to obtain a separate tax identification number. Completing this process can be time consuming, can require the assistance of an attorney, and can create additional fees and charges, none of which would have to be incurred if you didn't set up the living trust. That doesn't mean avoid using a trust. Just do it right.

❖    *Hype*: A living trust is the only document you really need.

❖    *Fact*: A living trust is never a substitute for a living will, health proxy, or HIPAA release, discussed in prior chapters. If your planning (not just the trust document) is done well, a living trust can, to a large degree, substitute for a will and power of attorney. However, you still need these other documents to ensure that no personal decisions, assets, or rights are missed.

Using a living trust as a substitute for a will does not work for many reasons. For example, a will is often necessary to designate a guardian for minor children. You need a will because there is no assurance that every asset you currently own will be owned by your living trust at your death. This disparity could occur because of the improper or incomplete transfer of assets, acquisitions for which there was inadequate time to complete a transfer to your trust, assets which could not be assigned, and finally, assets that you may not be aware of existing (e.g., a lottery winning, won just before you check out!). If you have a living trust, however, your will might be reduced to a much shorter document called a "pour-over will." This type of will provides that all assets under the will are simply to be transferred to (or poured-over into) your living trust. Nevertheless, a fairly complete will is sometimes advisable to authorize your executor to take the actions that might be necessary if circumstances change, so it could include a full range of powers and other rights given to this executor.

Living wills and health care proxies are essential to address medical decisions if you are incapacitated. You need these documents whether or not you also have a living trust. The living trust used in conjunction with these documents can provide an even greater level of protection and perhaps minimize the likelihood of a guardianship proceeding. That could be especially important if your COPD or other illnesses might likely result in a significant cognitive impairment or severe physical limitations.

A power of attorney also remains necessary. This designates someone to serve as your agent to handle legal, tax, and financial matters if you are disabled. You should have one even if you have a living trust to address assets and rights not transferred to the trust. It should be coordinated with the living trust to facilitate your agent transferring assets to the living trust if you are disabled.

❖  *Hype*: Living trusts are safer than wills.

❖  *Fact*: As explained earlier, especially in Chapter 4, living trusts are contracts and thus require a greater level of competency than that required to sign a will. Therefore, living trusts don't always prevent legal challenges—they may encourage them. If you are already experiencing cognitive impact because of your illness (e.g., mild dementia from oxygen deprivation during an exacerbation), the question as to the validity of a living trust must be evaluated by an attorney before you proceed to use this as a planning technique.

You can have the mental awareness (testamentary capacity) to sign a will but lack the required legal capacity to sign a living trust. A trust is a contract, so you must have the comprehension, understanding, and state of mind required to create one and have the assurance that it is (and will remain) legally binding. The standard that has been accepted by the law to sign a will has intentionally been made easier to enable people in extremis to sign wills. The standard to sign a will merely requires you to be aware of your descendants, the extent of your assets, and the fact that you are signing a document to bequeath those assets to the persons you name. If you are disabled or infirm, you may be legally incapable of signing a contract but still have sufficient capacity to sign a will. In such cases, a will might be the better, or even only, choice.

❖     *Hype*: Living trusts ensure confidentially; wills don't.

❖     *Fact*: If your estate is probated, or subject to a lawsuit, there is no assurance of confidentiality, and a living trust does not preclude probate or suit.

The claim that a living trust can enable you to minimize (not avoid) having your assets and wishes disclosed to the public is only a very small part of the story. Your will is a public document once probated. If your will contains a pour-over and is probated, the probate process may require that your living trust be recorded in the public record in a manner similar to recording your will. In addition, many states require the recording of a living trust in the same manner. If the living trust is challenged by a wannabe beneficiary, the trust might easily wind up in court records, which are open to the public. If there is a lawsuit, everything may become public. Thus, in some cases, there may be little or no additional confidentiality offered by a living trust. That doesn't mean you shouldn't have one; it just means that you should be aware of its limitations and focus on its real, not hyped, benefits.

❖     *Hype*: Living trusts will dramatically save on legal fees by avoiding probate.

❖     *Fact*: Living trusts don't save on legal fees; proper planning does.

Remember that your focus should be on what your living trust will do to protect you throughout the course of your illness. Whether or not you save legal fees on probate is not the primary question. Nevertheless, since this is a purported benefit, it can be addressed. Legal fees will be incurred on death whether a will or living trust is used. When a person with a living trust dies, the assets in that trust must still be transferred to the designated beneficiaries. Additional trusts may have to be set up (e.g., the bypass trust for tax benefits, trusts for minor children, a dynasty trust, etc.). Thus, whether assets pass through probate or under a living trust, steps will still have to be taken to transfer those assets. If the property is real estate, stocks or other assets, the paperwork may not be that different. In many cases, it is actually possible to probate an estate for far lower legal costs than many popular books and articles in financial publications indicate. Numbers like 5 percent to 10 percent, or more, of total assets are often suggested as typical costs and fees for probating an estate. In many instances, this is an exaggeration. The size of the estate often has little to do with the amount of work involved in the probate process. The nature of the assets, the cooperation of family members, and the organization of necessary financial and personal records are important factors in determining the extent of the legal work involved. Moreover, the particular probate court that will handle the estate can have a significant effect on the overall cost of a probate. Many probate (surrogate) court officials are extremely efficient, helpful, and professional, and this can dramatically reduce the cost and time involved. Regardless of whether your estate is taxable, a federal estate tax return will have to be filed to preserve a tax benefit called "portability." Using a living trust does nothing to reduce the costs of this filing.

❖   *Hype*: Living trusts avoid taxes.

❖   *Fact*: Most of the claimed tax benefits are a sales pitch!

From an income tax perspective, living trusts are characterized as "grantor trusts." This means that the income and expenses of the trust appear on your personal tax return as if the trust did not exist. For the 2012 federal tax return, only estates in excess of $5.12 million were subject to a federal estate tax. This figure may change in 2013. Although the future of the estate tax is uncertain, one thing is clear. If you might even possibly be subject to a federal estate tax, you can well afford to get proper legal advice to plan for it. You shouldn't be relying on a book or any marketing pitch. The only estate tax benefit from a living trust is when other planning techniques, in particular gift powers and other trusts (e.g., the bypass trust to benefit a surviving spouse while avoiding inclusion in his or her estate), are incorporated into a living trust. The living trust technique itself does not provide any tax benefit. These additional planning techniques are beyond the scope of this book and, with perhaps one exception, are identical to the planning techniques other taxpayers take. The key exception is that if your competency wanes as a result of your illness, you may not have the flexibility to revise your estate plan to address whatever form, if any, the estate tax will take in the future. You might in fact consider using a more sophisticated living trust document, one that gives considerably more flexibility to your trustees to modify tax aspects of your plan in the future if you are unable to do so, to establish and fund irrevocable trusts, and more.

## EXAMPLE

Assume that your living trust provides that the first $5.12 million of your assets could be transferred to a bypass trust to benefit your surviving spouse (for the sake of clarity, let's assume this is a wife), which will then not be taxed in her estate. On your wife's death, her $5.12 million estate is protected by the exemption of the $5.12 million available to her. The assets you transferred on your prior death to the bypass trust pass free of tax to your children on your wife's later death. By protecting your exclusion, and by using your wife's exemption, the estate tax is avoided through the provisions in your living trust. Your living trust, however, hasn't provided you any benefit that a will couldn't have similarly provided. Under current law if you simply left a portion or all of your estate outright to your wife (i.e., you did not use the bypass trust), your wife would be able to use the portion of your exemption that you did not use (called "portability").

# FOUR STAGES IN THE LIFE OF YOUR LIVING TRUST: HOW A LIVING TRUST WORKS

The best way to understand how a living trust works is to review the four stages in the lifecycle of a typical revocable living trust.

## ○ PHASE 1: FORMATION

After a complete review of your tax, estate, financial, and personal goals and status, a comprehensive plan should be formulated. When a revocable living trust is an appropriate component of this plan, you should retain a lawyer to draft the trust. The trust should be signed, witnessed, and notarized. Copies of the trust should be given to your professional advisers and family. Assets should then be transferred to your trust.

### ○ **PHASE 2: MANAGEMENT PRIOR TO YOUR BEING INCAPABLE OF ACTING AS TRUSTEE**

Manage the assets in your trusts as if they were your own, with one twist—transactions affecting trust assets will be completed in the name of the trust. You will sign trust checks and buy stock in your trust's name. However, if your illness has progressed significantly before you establish your living trust, you might have to skip this step and go to Phase 3. As noted earlier, having a co-trustee at Phase 2 is a great way to provide protections for you, keep you in control of your finances as long as possible, and ease the transition to Phase 3 when it becomes necessary. Having a co-trustee and consolidating all appropriate assets into your living trust may so simplify your financial and legal matters that it will significantly prolong the time period during which you can retain control of your affairs.

### ○ **PHASE 3: YOU BECOME INCAPABLE OF MANAGING YOUR AFFAIRS**

When you become incapable of serving as a trustee of your trust, your successor trustees will take over the management of your trust assets. Your agent, acting under your durable power of attorney, may transfer to your living trust any assets you own outside the trust (other than retirement assets). Your living trust should contain detailed provisions stating how and who should take over. The trust should make it clear how to determine that you are disabled so that your successor trustees can know when to take over. It should also indicate that if you recover, you can take back control of your financial management.

An important part of the disability provisions of your living trust is detailed instructions as to how you should be cared for in the event of disability. Many of the "form" trusts simply do not provide this type of personalized detail. Do you want to avoid being placed in a nursing home as long as possible? Do you have preferences for the type of health care facility in which you should be placed if it becomes absolutely necessary? If geographic preferences are important to you during your life, you should specify in your living trust that, in the event of your disability, you would wish to be placed in a facility located in a certain part of the country (perhaps near your family). If religious preferences are important, you may wish to specify that the health care facility be near a church, mosque, or synagogue so that you can attend services, or that the facility meets your religious dietary requirements. Do not assume that your trustees will know your preferences. Specifying such details may be critical, depending on who the trustees are. Details can also enable your trustees to respond to a challenge by your heirs as to the appropriateness of the decisions and expenditures they make.

## ○ PHASE 4: AFTER YOUR DEATH

On death, your trust becomes irrevocable and your successor trustees will carry out your wishes (e.g., funding a bypass trust). Any assets that were not already transferred to your trust (either by you when you formed the trust, at a later date by you, or by your agent under your durable power of attorney after your disability), can be transferred under what is known as a pour-over will. The key provision of this will provides that any assets that you may have owned at your death, which were not already in your trust, should be transferred (or poured over into) your living trust. Many different types of trusts can be incorporated into your living trust. Again, this type of planning is largely the same as for anyone and is not the focus of this book.

EXAMPLE • *COPD*
_____

With COPD you will likely have the capacity to handle your affairs for most, or all, of what should be a long life (normal life expectancy). So the need for using a revocable living trust is less critical then for other chronic illnesses, such as Alzheimer's, which assuredly leads to dementia and incompetency. That being said, the potential challenges COPD and potentially other health issues create for you, the smarter and safer approach is to create a funded revocable living trust long before you need it, and put in place within that document the safeguards to protect you from the "what ifs" that COPD might bring. There may in fact be periods of time, during a flare-up, or afterwards, where you may be somewhat disoriented or confused. Having most of your assets held in a living trust with a co-trustee that can manage matters, or even just help you, is a logical and prudent way to minimize the collateral problems that may occur. If you consolidate your financial and other assets in the trust (i.e., the fewest number of different banks, brokerage, and investment accounts feasible) and have duplicate monthly statements sent to an independent CPA to maintain records in Quicken or another personal finance program, you'll have a tremendous level of oversight. Should an acute situation occur, you have great protection.

If you want the Cadillac of security, name an independent trust company to serve as co-trustee with you. That can give you professional investment management, professional trustee services with personnel that have likely helped clients—scores if not hundreds of times, and more—through every issue you'll face. The combination of consolidation, institutional co-trustee, and independent CPA monitoring the trust is the gold standard. You might wish to start with less and save money, but bear in mind that protections put in place before you really need them are the most effective. There are other aspects to this as well. If the fatigue, mobility challenges, and other physical consequences of COPD make it difficult for you to run errands or devote the time to financial and other matters, creating the revocable living trust arrangement described above will not only protect you in the event that there are periods of time when you don't have the mindset or ability to handle these affairs, but it will also streamline to the maximum extent possible the time and physical effort you have to devote to these matters. Depending on your current status, and the future progression of your disease, one or both might prove helpful.

There is one final component that should be considered. Discuss with your attorney incorporating into your revocable living trust a mandate that once per year, and at some point quarterly or even more frequently, the independent or institutional trustee must (not should) have an independent care manager (i.e., not related, not involved in your regular care) meet you in your home and evaluate you and issue a written report to the independent trustee. A care manager may identify gaps in your medical care, problems in your home environment, your non-compliance with your recommended medical regimen, financial or elder abuse, and a host of other issues. Remember that all your professionals tend to meet you at preset appointments in their offices. Few if any ever see you in your living environment. A trained and experienced care manager can provide an important safeguard for you as a person that can otherwise fall through the cracks of the otherwise best devised revocable living trust an estate plan. While some or much of this might sound excessive to you, akin to using an M-1 tank to swat a fly, it is not. The incidence of financial and other abuse, the situations in which even close, successful, and supposedly caring family and friends have taken advantage of someone who is vulnerable, and realistically your health challenges make you more vulnerable than someone without health challenges, is common enough that you should err on the side of caution.

Perhaps most of the time, when you can manage your affairs, you might prefer to serve as sole trustee of your revocable trust. Consider the safeguards having a co-trustee can afford. Do you know if or when or how severe your next exacerbation will be? During an flare-up, will you need assistance? For how long and to what degree? Since there never can be any answers to these questions, err on the side of caution. As time goes on and your disabilities worsen, it will likely be helpful to have a co-trustee who can handle some of the administrative matters that you cannot handle, or which you might be able to handle but conserving your energy, or devoting your time instead to your recommended exercise regimen, would be better for you. A revocable trust might be the most appropriate tool to handle this contingency.

If you are married or have a partner, it might be assumed that your spouse or partner should be the obvious sole successor trustee; this is not always advisable. The burden of being a caregiver for you as your COPD progresses can be substantial, and providing assistance for the caregiver with a co-trustee, perhaps an institutional trustee than can relieve the caregiver of investment, distribution, check writing, and other burdens, may be ideal. If the caregiver is a friend and not a spouse, the insulation from claims by using an institutional trustee, especially in light of the other burdens the friend/caregiver carries, could be invaluable. If a bank or trust company serves as co-trustee, its involvement will insulate your partner or friend who serves as co-trustee from a variety of potential lawsuits.

The revocable trust should provide for a clear mechanism to determine if or when you should cease serving as trustee. If you are serving as a co-trustee with an institution and have funded the trust with most of your assets, that day will be put off as long as feasible and may never arrive. The language often used to accomplish this in many trust documents might be inappropriate to you in light of your COPD. Merely being "disabled" may not be a relevant criteria. You may be "disabled" from the date the trust is first signed, but still be quite capable of managing your financial and other affairs. Other disability triggers are inappropriate because even though you may be disabled during an exacerbation, following that exacerbation you may again be perfectly capable of managing your affairs. While some trusts use an on/off mechanism of providing that when the grantor/trustee recovers from a disability he or she will again resume being a trustee, this approach is also inadequate. The mechanisms may be too burdensome, the definitions may not address COPD, and timing issues may create problems. The specific definitions under which a successor trustee can demonstrate your inability to serve as trustee should be tailored to reflect the nuances of your illness, any cognitive impairment, and so on.

You should be encouraged to address with some detail the care and living arrangements you desire to provide guidance to the successor trustees. This might include personal details as to where and how you would like to live, and so forth.

## CHAPTER SUMMARY

This chapter has explored the revocable living trust, a document that can be the most important estate and financial planning tool to manage your affairs and ensure that you are protected throughout the course of your illness. However, as with all estate planning documents, you must carefully tailor this document to address your unique situation, and your experience of COPD.

# SAMPLE REVOCABLE LIVING TRUST
# PROVISIONS FOR THOSE WITH CHRONIC ILLNESS

Caution: This is merely an illustration and you must discuss the appropriate form to use with an attorney in your state.

> **[CAUTION:** *This is not a complete trust, just selected provisions. See www.laweasy.com for a complete sample document to discuss with your lawyer.*]

1. **Distributions [Selected provisions].**
   a. Distributions During Grantor's Lifetime - Grantor Not Disabled.
      i. During Grantor's lifetime when the Grantor is not disabled:
         1. The Trustee shall hold the Trust Estate, in trust, to pay or apply to or for the benefit of any one or more of the following persons: Grantor, Grantor's children (which shall include *CHILDREN NAMES, and any children born or legally adopted after the execution of this Trust Agreement, collectively "Children," individually "Child"), but not Grantor's grandchildren or later descendants (collectively these are referred to as "Recipients"). The net income of the Trust shall be applied in amounts, whether equal or unequal, as the Trustee (or the Independent Trustee where applicable), in the exercise of discretion, may consider desirable for the health, education, support, or maintenance, to maintain the Recipient's in accordance with the Standard for Payment defined below. The judgment of the Trustee, as to the propriety and amount of such payment, shall be conclusive.
         2. It is the express desire of the Grantor that the Trustee apply income liberally, and primarily for the care of Grantor and in a manner to maintain Grantor's historic lifestyle and activities to the extent feasible and practical in light of Grantor's current and future health status. These decisions shall be made without concern for the retention of any monies for future or remainder beneficiaries.
         3. The Trustee may accumulate any of the net income not paid or applied for the benefit of the Recipients, and add it to the principal of this Trust at least annually and thereafter to hold, administer, and dispose of it as a part of the Trust Estate.
      ii. Distributions During Grantor's Life - Grantor Disabled.
         1. During Grantor's disability, as defined below, the Trustee shall administer the Trust Estate for the care of Grantor, and shall expend any amounts of Trust income or principal as the Trustee, in the exercise of discretion, shall deem necessary or advisable in accordance with the following provisions.
         2. During any disability of the Grantor, the Grantor directs that the no restrictions shall apply as to distributions to or for the benefit of Grantor. Grantor directs that during Grantor's disability:
            a. Grantor directs that Grantor have the best medical and health care provided to Grantor and that the Trustee shall distribute Trust income and principal accordingly. The term "best" shall be defined, to the extent feasible and applicable based on the caliber of medical care that Grantor sought prior to being deemed disabled under the provisions of this Trust, adjusted to reflect the current status of Grantor's health. Notwithstanding the foregoing, the Trustee is directed to pay for and to the extent feasible actively seek out experimental and new medical therapies to help Grantor's condition, including but not limited to alternative treatments that have received positive reviews in medical literature.
            b. Grantor directs that every effort reasonable be made to enable Grantor to continue to reside in Grantor's personal residence for as long as practical, and that every reasonable effort be made to accommodate Grantor's health care needs in such home rather than relocating to a health care facility.
            c. In the event that Grantor must be relocated to any nursing or health care facility, Grantor directs that every effort possible be made that any such facility:
               i. Be operated under *RELIGIOUS PREFERENCE auspices.
               ii. Have *DESCRIBE food service facilities, and where possible have, or be within reachable distance to a *RELIGION house of worship.

d. Notwithstanding anything in this Trust to the contrary, any restrictions on distributions provided in the provision below governing "Distributions To A Person Under A Disability," shall not apply to restrict any distributions to Grantor when Grantor is disabled, or following any period of Grantor's disability *[Note: Many trust documents include additional restrictions on distributions to a beneficiary who is disabled. In this context, those would be generic provisions to apply in the event an heir who receives funds from the trust is disabled. Those provisions would not be tailored to address your situation, so they are made inapplicable to you].*

3. Short Duration Disability from Which Recovery Is Anticipated.

a. Because Grantor is living with COPD *DESCRIBE YOUR STATUS AND ANY OTHER HEALTH CHALLENGE OR CHRONIC ILLNESS, it is anticipated that periodically Grantor may suffer a short term flare-up or hospitalization. The Grantor directs that, barring an emergency situation which cannot await Grantor's recuperation or recovery from such attack or exacerbation, that the disability provisions in this Trust shall not be applied so long as the period for which it is anticipated that Grantor will not be able to reasonably participate in the management of this Trust shall be less than Thirty (30) days. This condition shall be referred to as an "Ignored Disability."

b. However, in the event that an institutional cotrustee is serving and such institutional trustee *[Note: Modify if you are not using an institution, but consider if you wish to grant this authority to a non-institutional trustee]* determines in its absolute discretion that Grantor must be replaced to address an important or emergency situation.

c. In the event of Grantor being subject to an Ignored Disability, a confirmation by any of Grantor's attending physicians in writing that Grantor is subject to an Ignored Disability as defined above shall suffice to confirm such status.

4. Determination of Grantor's Disability.

a. The Grantor shall be deemed to be disabled when Grantor is unable to manage Grantor's affairs and property effectively for reasons such as mental illness, mental deficiency, physical illness or disability, advanced age, chronic use of drugs, chronic intoxication, confinement, kidnapping, detention by a foreign power or disappearance, or for any other reason allowable by statute or law. Grantor expressly states that Grantor presently has COPD *OTHER CHRONIC ILLNESS and has the following conditions and symptoms *DESCRIBE SYMPTOMS. Further, Grantor anticipates that *FUTURE SYMPTOMS are likely to occur. So long as Grantor, with the assistance and guidance of the Institutional Cotrustee *[Note: If you don't use an institutional Cotrustee, modify and rethink this]* is able to reasonably participate in the management and decision making under this trust, regardless of *DESCRIBE ACCEPTABLE LIMITATIONS, shall remain a Cotrustee hereunder and shall not be deemed disabled. *[Note: The objective is to tailor the definition of "disability" so that you are only replaced as a trustee when you really should be. Unless you address the nuances of your situation, that decision won't be made at the appropriate time].*

b. In addition to any other method acceptable to any third party relying upon the effectiveness of the appointment of any Trustee or successor Trustee, or any method allowed by law, it shall be deemed conclusive proof that the appointment of such person is effective upon a written statement being executed by each of Grantor's neurologist [OTHER SPECIALIST] and primary care physician or internist has become physically or mentally incapacitated, regardless of cause and regardless of whether or not there has been an adjudication of incompetence, mental illness, or need for a committee, conservator, guardian, or other personal representative.

5. Successor Trustee When Grantor Disabled. Where Grantor is disabled, the next person selected from the provision below Additional or Successor Trustee shall serve as Cotrustee in place of Grantor. *[Note: This is one of the most important decisions. Who should be in charge of your trust when you cannot serve as trustee or co-trustee?].*

6. Grantor's Recovery from Disability. The Grantor shall be deemed to have recovered from any such disability when the other then serving Trustee receives written certification from Two (2) physicians regularly attending the Grantor, at least One (1) of which physicians is board certified in the specialty most closely associated with the alleged disability, that the Grantor is no longer physically or mentally incapacitated, and that Grantor is again able to manage his or her own financial affairs. The Trustee shall not be liable to any person, including Grantor, for the removal of the Grantor as a Trustee, if he or she acted in good faith on the

certificates obtained in accordance with this provision. Upon such recovery, Grantor shall serve as a Cotrustee with any trustee theretofore serving. *[Note: This is a commonly used provision but may not apply in the context of your situation as once your cognitive ability has declined to the point where you are not able to serve as a Cotrustee, this provision will never apply. In the event your illness is marked by intermittent attacks or exacerbations, this cumbersome process of declaring you "disabled" and then "recovered" makes little sense to repeat].*

**2. Charitable Bequest Following Grantor's Death.** The Trustee shall distribute an amount equal to AMOUNT Dollars ($*.00) to CHARITY NAME from the Trust Estate following the death of Grantor. The Trustee shall have the power and discretion to fund this gift wholly or partly in cash or kind, and to select the assets which shall constitute this gift. However, the Trustee shall determine the value all assets so selected, and assets comprising the Trust Estate. *[Note: Give consideration to making some gift to the charity that is devoted to serving those with COPD and funding research to cure that disease. Even a small gift will enlarge the roster of those making such commitments and may thereby enhance overall fund-raising efforts, even current fund-raising].*

**3. Grantor's Investment Goals for Trust Estate.**

a. Grantor hereby communicates Grantor's general investment goals to the Trustee. Grantor states that *DESCRIBE INVESTMENT POLICY. *[Note: See Chapter 4 for a discussion of investment planning for you in light of your chronic illness. Your investment goals may differ from those of someone without your health considerations. But it is impossible without further details and planning to understand how it should differ. If you establish a living trust your financial adviser should help you address this].*

b. In formulating any investment policy or making any decision with respect to any assets, and assets relating to any closely held or family business and investment interests, it is Grantor's direction and intent that such interests may be held in the reasonable judgment of the Trustee. *[Note: If you have a business you want retained, it should be addressed].*

c. Grantor expressly directs the Trustee endeavor to retain Grantor's personal residence located at HOME ADDRESS if feasible for Grantor to remain there. Grantor does not make this an absolute prohibition against sale in light of the possibility that Grantor may benefit from residing in an assisted living or other facility. Grantor recommends that the Trustee consider Grantor's strong desire, but not mandate, that Grantor remain in said home, the modifications previously made to the home to accommodate Grantor and an future aide or companion, and other factors.

d. Grantor expressly authorizes, as an exception to the Prudent Investor Act, the Trustees to invest a portion of the trust estate in gift annuities provided through the auspices of CHARITY NAME even if these gift annuities are not an optimal or advisable investment allocation. Grantor authorizes the Trustees to consider Grantor's personal goals of benefit such charity in its research efforts to find a cure for CHRONIC DISEASE and other efforts through the use of gift annuities. *[Note: Gift annuities can be an important source of fund-raising for many of the charities devoted to combating various chronic illnesses. However, a trustee may be precluded from purchasing such annuities by the Prudent Investor Act, a law which directs how trustees should invest trust assets. If you wish to permit this a specific exception to protect and direct the trustees may be necessary].*

**4. Trustee Decision Making and Authority.**

a. Any authority, discretion or power granted to or conferred upon the Cotrustees by this Trust may be exercised by any such Trustees who shall be acting under this Trust Agreement at such time, or by such one of them who shall be so designated by an instrument in writing executed by any other Trustee.

b. Any one of the Co-trustees acting alone and without any requirement for joint action is authorized and permitted to complete alone any ministerial and administrative act, including but not limited to routine banking, investment, and brokerage transactions, except that when an institutional trustee is serving as a Cotrustee hereunder only such Institutional Cotrustee shall make investment decisions. It is the express intent of this provision to permit the Grantor when not disabled to continue to manage routine matters within the Grantor's purview, and to permit the Cotrustee other than the Grantor to manage routine matters when the Grantor is subject to an Ignored Disability.

c. This paragraph, however, shall not be interpreted or applied in a manner that violates any restriction in the provisions governing an Independent Trustee, person under legal obligation. Therefore, where the provisions governing an Independent Trustee apply, the Independent Trustee alone may make any such decisions or take any actions reasonably within the purview of such Independent Trustee.

d. Where there are more than Two (2) Trustees at any time the decision of a majority of them shall control and shall be binding on all of the Trustees.

e. If Two (2) or more Trustees are acting hereunder, the following provisions shall apply where the context permits:

i. The corporate or institutional Trustee shall have custody of the Trust Estate and of the books and records of the Trust.

ii. With respect to any matter as to which the Trustees have joint authority, a Trustee from time to time may delegate any or all of that Trustee's rights, powers, duties, and discretion as Trustee to the other Trustee, with the consent of the latter.

iii. The Trustee may establish bank accounts and it shall be assumed unless specified otherwise in the application for such account that checks or drafts may be drawn on, or withdrawals made from, any such account on the individual signature of either Trustee.

iv. A Trustee shall be presumed to have approved a proposed act or decision to refrain from acting if that Trustee fails to indicate approval or disapproval therefore within Thirty (30) days after written Notice requesting approval.

## CHAPTER 11

# CHARITABLE GIVING

## INTRODUCTION TO CHARITABLE GIVING AND YOUR FINANCIAL AND ESTATE PLAN

PEOPLE CONTRIBUTE TO CHARITY primarily for personal reasons. Usually those personal reasons are to help a cause and goal they are concerned about, for example, promoting research to rid the world of a chronic illness, such as COPD. But charitable giving can also be tailored to help specific needs for you or your family, as long as there is no personal benefit that would jeopardize your income tax deduction. When helping a particular person along with benefiting a cause important to you are combined, the personal gratification and benefits of charitable giving can outweigh the tax and financial rewards (but obviously those benefits should be maximized to the extent not inconsistent with your personal goals). When you, or a family member or loved one, is facing the challenges of COPD, commonly used charitable giving techniques can be tailored to address your needs, or the needs of that specific person, while simultaneously helping the causes of treating or finding a cure for COPD. It does not require new-fangled charitable giving techniques, just molding traditional charitable planning to personal circumstances. This requires an understanding of your particular illness, and the tax and charitable giving techniques available. With tax laws so in flux, bear in mind that any planning idea should be reviewed with a professional adviser and tailored to address any recent developments in the law.

If you have COPD, you may feel disempowered. Structuring a charitable gift, even if it doesn't make an immediate difference for you (or your loved who is living with COPD), will give you the feeling that you are making a difference. This can empower you and make you feel that you are doing something constructive to combat COPD. Typically, a parent's or sibling's first reaction to your diagnosis is to ask how they can help. Suggest a donation.

EXAMPLE

Research is demonstrating that susceptibility to developing COPD may be caused by genes. Alpha-1 antitrypsin deficiency is the most common known genetic risk factor for COPD, and the information retrieved from investigating Alpha-1 Antitrypsin Deficiency has led researchers to learn about the biological processes that lead to COPD. As many as 3 percent of individuals with COPD have undetected alpha-1 antitrypsin deficiency. It is also well known that not all smokers develop COPD, suggesting that susceptibility to developing COPD has a genetic basis. But the information researchers have learned from alpha-1 antitrypsin deficiency has brought up questions as to what are the other genetic risk factors for COPD. Scientific researchers are about to begin an investigation to find the genes that cause a susceptibility to developing COPD. The COPD Foundation is one of many fine charities funding and pursuing this goal. If there are other COPD research efforts you might prefer, Google "COPD Research" and choose from any of the great organizations or causes.

## DONATE APPRECIATED STOCKS FOR GIFT ANNUITIES

This is a common staple of charitable planning. But while many donors will simply donate securities with no benefit other than a charitable deduction, for someone living with a COPD, this may not be enough. For you, cash flow for living expenses and medical costs are likely a significant concern. If you sell appreciated securities, you will pay a capital gains tax. You will then have to invest and manage the proceeds, which may not be practical for you as your chronic illness progresses. If instead, you donate appreciated securities to a charity in exchange for a gift annuity, this will provide you with a charitable contribution deduction (which will vary based on age) and cash flow in the form of an annuity for the rest of your life. This not only provides an income tax benefit but also eliminates the need for you to continue to manage the assets. Your investment and cash flow are on autopilot. If you're struggling with other demands and stress related to your COPD, having a portion of your portfolio converted to a tax-advantaged annuity might be appropriate. But unlike a mere commercial annuity, a gift annuity with a charitable organization funding research to find a cure for your illness provides an important additional benefit. But you should be careful about how much you can commit to gift annuities (or charitable remainder trusts, CRTs) because once the gift/donation is made, you cannot access the principal in the event of an emergency. If your finances are "tight" you should evaluate with a financial planner whether a charitable gift annuity is affordable to you. This is because the determinations of how much you can get paid will reflect a significant gift following your life expectancy to the charity. That's a good thing and why a charitable gift annuity to a charity serving those with COPD entices you. But the calculated amount to the charity will reduce what you can get paid when compared to a commercial annuity.

## FAMILY MEMBERS CAN USE INSURANCE TO BENEFIT YOU AND A CHARITY

To help your goals, a healthy spouse or family member can often use life insurance planning to benefit both you and a charity.

### EXAMPLE

Janice Gordon has two sons and a daughter. Her daughter Francine was diagnosed with COPD at age 42. Janice is adamant that her will bequeath assets equally as she does not want to create any animosity or jealously among the children. Janice is especially concerned about keeping the peace because her sons have been wonderfully supportive and helpful of her daughter since her diagnosis. However, Janice realistically understands that Francine may not be able to work to her regular retirement age, and that limiting her work time might give her more time to devote to self-care to deal with her COPD. Janice is a bit concerned that COPD might undermine Francine's ability to maintain what Janice believes is an adequate lifestyle. Janice's will simply leave all assets to her children equally. Janice establishes an irrevocable (cannot be changed) life insurance trust that purchases a $1 million universal insurance policy on her life. This trust is designed to help support and supplement Francine. If Francine marries and has children, on Francine's death, the funds in the trust will be distributed to her children. Janice feels this is important because she does not believe Francine will have the capacity to earn enough to leave an inheritance to her children and cannot easily obtain life insurance because of her COPD and other health issues if Francine dies without children, the COPD Foundation is named as the beneficiary of the remaining insurance proceeds.

## IMPLEMENT A REVOCABLE LIVING TRUST WITH A CHARITABLE REMAINDER

For anyone living with COPD, establishing a revocable living trust to manage assets as the disease leads to disability is an important estate, financial, and personal planning step, as described in Chapter 10. If you establish a revocable trust to provide for the management of your assets, consider permitting some amount of charitable donations by the trustees, including the possible purchase of gift annuities from designated charities devoted to helping those with COPD. This is important because if contributions and even gift annuities aren't addressed specifically, the trustee may be precluded from taking these steps, or may be so concerned about violating his or her fiduciary duties as trustee, that he or she might refrain from doing so even if not absolutely prohibited by law.

## CRT TO BENEFIT YOURSELF

If you're a business owner, and it is getting more difficult for you to manage the business as your COPD progresses, an exit strategy will eventually become necessary. You could donate part of the business to a charitable remainder trust ("CRT"), which could then sell the business without your incurring a capital gains tax. The proceeds can be reinvested and the CRT would pay you a periodic annuity for life. This annuity could cover a significant portion of your medical and living expenses. On your death, the money remaining in the CRT will be given to the charity you've selected, or to a surviving spouse if you wish, and thereafter to the charity. This is a traditional application of a CRT technique to accomplish a number of your estate and financial planning goals. The timing of the sale could be based on the progression of your chronic illness, not market forces for maximizing return. The charity you select could be one whose mission is to further research or provide assistance for those with COPD. The benefits of this application of a CRT could be substantial. If capital gains rates rise in the future, the benefits could even be greater.

### EXAMPLE

Adam wants to provide for the protection of his wife Dana who suffers from COPD. Adam contemplates donating $1 million of stock that he has held for many years and that has appreciated substantially over its $150,000 purchase price. Adam has already engaged in considerable estate planning to benefit his and Dana's children and feels that is important to support the several charities funding COPD research following his and Dana's deaths. Adam is hopeful that setting up a CRT for these charities will encourage others to make major current and deferred gifts, thereby hastening the research that will hopefully help his wife. Adam decides to establish an inter vivos (while he is alive) charitable remainder trust (CRT) for both himself and Dana. Both Adam and Dana will have current interests in the CRT. A current income tax deduction will be permitted, based on the present value of the future interest the charities named will receive. A deduction is permitted because the rights of the charities are fixed in a manner that conforms to the tax law requirements for a current deduction. A specified payout must occur in each year (or more frequent period if required in the trust). No additional payments may be made to Adam or Dana, other than those fixed in the CRT document when it is established. Properly structured, this will also qualify for a gift tax marital deduction (because Adam is making a gift to Dana through the annuity payments she will receive during her lifetime). However, should Dana face an emergency, the trustees cannot distribute principal of the trust to her, so Adam has made sure there are other resources for her in the event of an emergency. After the death of both Adam and Dana, the principal remaining in the trust is to be distributed to the named charities to establish a research grant in their memory.

The various charities are named the remainder beneficiary of the CRT. Adam and Dana can also reserve the right in their CRT to name new charities in their wills in case new discoveries or developments change the landscape of who they believe can best tackle COPD issues in future.

## MARITAL GIFT FOLLOWED BY SPOUSAL CRT

If your spouse is living with COPD, you can gift appreciated assets, such as growth stock mutual funds, to your spouse. Your spouse can then establish a CRT for his or her benefit, and contribute the appreciated mutual funds to the CRT. The CRT can continue the current investments as long as necessary. At the appropriate time, the mutual funds can be sold and the proceeds reinvested (free of any capital gains tax) in income oriented funds. The income from the CRT's revised asset allocation strategy can be used to pay your spouse an annuity for life. Your spouse won't have to address management of the assets, provided he or she uses the services of a trustee.

An income tax charitable contribution deduction could be realized on your joint income tax return when the CRT is initially formed and the mutual funds contributed. Your spouse can have an annuity payment made monthly or quarterly for the rest of his or her life. After your spouse dies, the designated charity will receive the remaining assets held in the CRT. But the charity will realize intangible benefits from the date the CRT is initially formed in that it will be able to reflect the commitment in its efforts to solicit other donors. This can boost fund-raising efforts for the charity, something likely to be of significant importance to you. This approach may also be used to maximize the distributions to your spouse. If the chronically ill spouse has COPD, for example, her life span may not be adversely affected so that the support of the CRT will be needed for a substantial time period. In such instances, a unitrust that can provide more inflation protection may be warranted. In a unitrust, a percentage of the fair value of the trust assets each year is used to determine the payment (instead of a fixed percentage of the initial trust assets determining the annuity). If the value of the assets increases over time, the value of the payment will as well. The theory is that this increase will help the payment maintain its purchasing power even in the face of inflation.

If your spouse is living with COPD, establishing a trust for his or her benefit can be an important planning step because there is no guarantee that you can care for this person indefinitely. While it is often assumed that the spouse with the chronic illness will die first, the caregiver may succumbs first because of other health issues and the stress of caregiving. Caregiving for a spouse with COPD, can be very difficult. Often, it involves physical as well as emotional stress to the caregiver, especially if he or she is elderly. When such physical support is prolonged, the physical consequences to the caregiver can be debilitating.

EXAMPLE

Cindy's husband Sam has COPD. Cindy wants to provide financial protection and management (in the event something happens to her) for Sam for his life, but on his demise, Cindy wants to benefit charities providing services to those families with a member living with COPD. Cindy establishes an inter vivos (while she is alive) marital trust (QTIP) for Sam. Sam has a current interest in the trust. No current income tax deduction is permitted for the future interest the charity will receive after Sam's death. No deduction is permitted because the rights of the charities are not created in a manner that conforms to the tax law requirements for a current income tax deduction. To protect Sam, the trust may pay any necessary amounts of the trust principal (assets) to Sam, or for his benefit, during Sam's lifetime. A trust company is named as co-trustee. This ensures that if Sam can no longer fully participate in the management of the trust, a bank will provide for whatever financial and other services he needs. Properly structured, this trust will qualify for a gift tax marital deduction when Cindy establishes it. During Sam's lifetime, all income must be distributed at least annually to him or for his benefit. In addition, should Sam face an emergency, the trustees could distribute principal for the benefit of Sam as they see fit. On Sam's demise, the principal remaining in the trust is to be distributed to the named charities as the final recipient ("remainder beneficiary"). There will not be any current charitable contribution deduction. However, on Sam's death, although the value of the entire trust will be included in his taxable estate, there will be an equal and offsetting charitable contribution deduction. This approach ensures flexibility in case Sam lives for many years or faces financial needs that are not presently anticipated.

## CLT TO BENEFIT TARGET CHARITY AND A CHILD WITH CHRONIC ILLNESS

A charitable lead trust ("CLT") is a trust designed to benefit a charity and at the same time provide a future gift (inheritance) to your child (or other heir) at a substantially reduced gift tax cost. When you establish a CLT, the designated charity receives an annuity payment (the greater the percentage payment, the more substantial the tax benefit), for the number of years you specify (the greater the number of years, the greater the tax benefit). Thereafter, the assets in the trust will be distributed to the child (or other heir you named). This approach can be a tremendous way to help fund research to find a cure for COPD that your child or other heir is living with while ensuring a safety net for the child's financial future. It's also a great way for you to feel that you are fighting COPD proactively.

This approach may be viable for some people diagnosed with COPD, but not for others. A major factor will be the age at which your loved one is diagnosed. For example, if your child is diagnosed in his or her 40s or even perhaps 50s and you have sufficient wealth to make a plan like this viable, a charitable lead trust could be used over a long enough period to minimize gift taxes, benefit a charity conducting COPD research, and provide a financial safety net for your child (or other heir). COPD is often diagnosed when a patient is in his or his or her 40s to 60s, which at the younger ages may permit this type of long-term CLT planning. However, when diagnosed in someone much older, the time span between initial diagnosis and the need for funds may be too short for the CLT technique to provide much benefit.

## OTHER CHARITABLE PLANNING TIPS

When you or a loved one plans a charitable gift, consider the pitfalls and problems that these gifts can raise with your accountant and financial planner. The list below is not all inclusive and barely touches upon the complexity. The take-home message is that many charitable planning transactions have complex tax and other twists that are best dealt with by a professional.

### *Loss Property*

Do not donate assets that have declined in value. Consider transferring or selling the loss property (e.g., a rental property you purchased for $300,000 that is now worth only $200,000) now to take advantage of the losses, or gift the loss property to a spouse who may be able to take advantage of it later. Be sure not to use this for funding charitable gifts since the loss in the asset won't be realized. If you sell the property at a loss and donate the proceeds to charity, you may get some tax benefits from the loss.

### *Testamentary Bequests*

Another common trap is the manner in which a testamentary bequest is structured. Too often a bequest is assumed to be simple, when in fact, a host of complex issues can be raised.

#### EXAMPLE

Jim Fitzgerald has two adult children, a son, Thomas, and a daughter, Sandy, who is in her 50s and is living with COPD. While Jim would prefer to leave assets equally to his two children on his death, he is not certain this is fair, given the uncertainty about the progression of Sandy's COPD. After reviewing the matter with the family, Jim opts for the following dispositive scheme in his will: 55 percent to Sandy, 40 percent to Thomas, and 5 percent to a well-known national hospital that has several cutting edge programs to deal with treating patients living with COPD.

When Jim discusses this plan with his attorney, a couple of important issues are raised. While there is a likelihood that Sandy will need more financial assistance than Thomas, that really cannot be known for certain: The progression of Sandy's disease is unknown, and there are new therapies being developed. Just as importantly, Jim's attorney points out that there is no certainty that Thomas will not face some type of financial, health, or other adversity. Finally, Jim's attorney explains that if a percentage of his estate is left to charity, the will and financial reporting will have to be submitted to the state's attorney general's office to comply with state law. The attorney further points out the valuation issues that can arise if a percentage of an estate is left to charity. Jim anticipates that the family vacation home in the country will be kept by both Thomas and Sandy, for personal use for them and their children. For estate tax purposes, the children have the incentive to value this house as low as possible to minimize estate tax costs. However, the hospital, as an independent charitable beneficiary, is obligated to ensure that fair market values are used. The greater the value of the vacation home the greater the charity's 5 percent interest. This disparity in goals could create some friction. The combination of these and other issues, the attorney explains, makes a donation of a percentage of the estate potentially problematic. So Jim settles on the following dispositive scheme: A fixed dollar bequest of $500,000 in his will to the hospital to be used to develop programming and facilities to serve those living with COPD. The remaining estate is divided three ways: 40 percent to Thomas and 40 percent to Sandy, with each bequest to be structured in a separate trust designed to meet the specific needs of each child. The remaining 20 percent of the estate is to be distributed to a family "pot" trust, which can benefit any child or grandchild based on need. The family trust will likely be divided into two components: GST exempt and non exempt. The children and the charity all benefit from this revised plan.

## *Select IRD Assets for Charitable Gifts*

If you have a chronic illness, consider the types of assets you own. To the extent that you have accounts receivable, individual retirement accounts (IRAs, but not Roth IRAs), or other assets that are subject to income taxation under the income in respect of a decedent rules ("IRD"), you may want to consider bequeathing these assets to a charity because the charity won't have to recognize the income tax, and you will get a reduction in estate values. These are the most advantageous assets to use.

## LEGAL CONSTRAINTS ON CHARITABLE GIVING

Consider revising durable powers of attorney to expressly permit your agents to make gifts to a charity or a particular cause. Similarly, if you own interests in LLCs or corporations that you might wish to donate, be certain while you are able to negotiate and implement a change, that the entity's governing documents are modified to remove restrictions on charitable transfers, or to at least permit them with certain conditions.

## CHAPTER SUMMARY

You don't have to be a millionaire to make a donation that has an impact on a COPD charitable cause important to you. As this chapter suggests, most people living with COPD have long lives and successful careers, and good charitable planning can encourage others to give. Giving (to any degree and in any amount) to charities fighting COPD, researching new therapies, and helping those facing the challenges of COPD, can accomplish a host of important goals and should be part of your estate and financial plan.

## CHAPTER 12

# OTHER CONSIDERATIONS

## PLANNING FOR FAMILY MEMBERS

IF YOU HAVE COPD, your planning should ideally be considered in light of the estate and financial planning of your family members. Coordination as a family unit in many cases can provide better results for all. This is not always an easy task to accomplish, but generally the benefits outweigh the challenges. This doesn't mean that your parents and children all have to use the same advisers, it just means some open communication is necessary. This discussion provides an overview of some of the points to evaluate.

### SHOULD YOU RESIGN AS AGENT AND FIDUCIARY UNDER FAMILY DOCUMENTS?

The challenges of living with COPD vary considerably from person to person. Your age of diagnosis, the resources that you have available to help (financial and other), whether or not you have other health issues, and so forth, all affect your experience of COPD. For many with COPD, at some point it will become prudent to simplify their lives and minimize the financial, legal, and other responsibilities they have to minimize stress, conserve energy, and free up time to devote to self-care. So, at some point, COPD may affect your ability, or perhaps just the appropriateness, of your serving as an agent, trustee, or executor under their estate planning documents. The simplest and least costly approach to address this is to inform loved ones and close friends that named you to remove your name the next time they revise their documents. If you are already serving, it may be preferable for you to execute documents resigning (releasing you from serving) as agent, trustee, or executor. This will be far easier than someone at a later date having to demonstrate you are not able to serve and have you formally removed.

EXAMPLE

Uncle Joe, now age 85, has always trusted and relied upon you and named you as agent under his power of attorney to help him out. You were diagnosed about 10 years ago with COPD and after a recent exacerbation realize the burdens of helping Uncle Joe will detract from your ability to take care of matters you need to address. The prudent step would be to advise Uncle Joe to have his attorney revise his power of attorney and name a different agent.

## HOW YOUR CHRONIC ILLNESS AFFECTS YOUR SPOUSE'S/PARTNER'S OR PARENTS' WILLS

Your chronic illness may have an important effect on how your spouse, partner, parent, or other family members' wills should be prepared if they are naming you a beneficiary. There are a few things they should to take into consideration in their planning as it pertains to you. Unless you are substantially well off, it may be advisable, given the often draining financial cost of medical treatment and the possibility of long-term health care costs, for your family to leave any bequests to you in the form of a Special Needs Trust ("SNT"). An SNT can be set up to provide you with benefits only in excess of what state and other governmental benefits won't cover. These extra or "special" needs payment restrictions should safeguard these inherited assets from undermining your qualification for vital government programs. It should also safeguard these inherited assets for your use.

Regardless of your financial position, loved ones considering bequeathing you money should tailor trusts to hold the assets they leave you. Those trusts should not consist of only the boilerplate trust provisions often used. They ideally should incorporate some of the suggestions made in preceding chapters of this book for planning for COPD. If possible, you should probably be a co-trustee of any trust family members or others establish for your benefit, unless of course your cognitive impact has risen to a degree that makes this impractical. Special precautions may have to be taken if an incremental goal is to prevent those assets from being taxed in your estate. For example, your family member's estate planner may limit your right as a co-trustee to withdraw money from the trust solely to maintain your standard of living (an "ascertainable standard" in tax jargon) and take other steps. Since these are complex tax matters, your family member's advisers will need to address them. They are beyond the scope of this book. The key point is that coordinating family planning on a big picture basis can provide more control for you, preservation of assets from nursing home and other health care costs while still protecting you, or tax savings if applicable.

KEY

> 🔑      In many situations, depending on which chronic illness you have and the extent to which it currently affects you, there is no reason for you not to be a co-trustee and be actively involved in a trust a family member sets up for you.

## PLANNING FOR YOUR PARTNER/SPOUSE

If you are married or have a partner, planning for chronic illness should also include special consideration for the role that a partner or spouse fulfills as caregiver. Caregiving requires time and emotional capital, and can take a substantial toll on the caregiver. Studies have reported that about one-third of caregivers have high blood pressure, about one-third have high cholesterol, about 15 percent suffer from chronic headaches, about 15 percent have persistent sleep disorders, and nearly one-fifth have mood disorders. These facts need to be kept in mind when discussing basic estate planning decisions. For example, when evaluating whom to name as trustee of your revocable living trust, consider naming an institutional co-trustee (or other co-trustee) to ease the administrative burden on your caregiver. Too often those planning for someone with a chronic illness focus only on the person living with the illness, with no regard for the impact that illness has on loved ones and caregivers. This also supports a more aggressive recommendation for you to name an institutional co-fiduciary whenever practicable.

Partners or spouses should also revise their estate planning documents to ensure that any assets left to you are left in a trust to provide for a management structure as discussed above. In some situations a special needs trust may be advisable.

# Religious Considerations

Few lawyers address religion in their legal documents. However, when dealing with the life and death decisions discussed in Chapter 8 on living wills and health care proxies, charitable giving discussed in Chapter 11, and a host of other issues mentioned in this book, religious considerations are important for many people. Many turn to their religious faith in the face of adversity. Because you are living with COPD, you may well find solace in your religious roots. Even if you have not, perhaps your loved ones have. In either case, you might wish to address religious considerations with your attorney. There are many provisions, documents, and planning steps that might warrant modification to address religious concerns, and some are discussed below. It is not a comprehensive listing, but a sampling of issues and situations that you might wish to discuss with a religious adviser as well as with your estate planning professionals.

## SELECTING FIDUCIARIES

If you are seeking to imbue your estate planning documents with religious values or to transmit a particular religious heritage to a child or other heir, one of the most important decisions you can make is to select fiduciaries that have one or all of the following: knowledge of the particular faith, affiliation or observance of that faith themselves, and/or sensitivity to the specific needs of the heirs in light of the religious goals and objectives. In many instances, the person that best fits these criteria will not be the person best suited to handle investment and other fiduciaries responsibilities. Your selection of fiduciaries will have a profound impact on your ability to transmit values. The context of fiduciaries should not only include trustees, but also agents under a power of attorney in the event a chronic illness or other incapacity results in the power being the operative document for many years.

## DISTRIBUTIONS

The agents (under your power of attorney) and fiduciaries (executors and trustees under your will) should be given guidance and granted legal authority to disburse funds for religious education (e.g., supplemental religious education or private school), religious travel (pilgrimages to holy sites), charitable giving (to meet your religious obligations and, when appropriate, to inculcate a core religious value in heirs), and other purposes consistent with your religious goals. Boilerplate distribution provisions in many documents just won't suffice.

## CHARITABLE GIVING

Every religion advocates the virtues of charity, but charitable giving can be tailored to reflect the unique nuances of your faith. While many religions mandate tithing a certain percentage of income or assets to charity, others provide more specific standards.

## HEROIC MEASURES

Perhaps the single phrase in all of estate planning that has more potential for religious repercussions than any other is the mandate in a living will or health care proxy that "no heroic measures" be taken. There are, apart from the obvious ambiguities of this phrase, a host of moral and ethical considerations that anyone with religious sensitivity needs to address. Some people, depending on their religious convictions or upbringing, assume that they can never withdraw life support without violating their religious standards. Sometimes, this interpretation may be incorrect, but in many cases the issues involved are a complex web of religious and medical decision making. These types of decisions can be fraught with religious nuance that cannot easily be resolved.

For example, the Catholic Church does not mandate that a person be kept alive no matter what. A Catholic can decide to avoid overly invasive and experimental procedures, but not ordinary means of care. "Ordinary means" could include feeding someone, making certain they have air to breathe, and so on. According to the Catholic Church, then, a patient must continue to receive ordinary care; otherwise, those denying that care are effectively acting to cause the patient's death. The extraordinary means go beyond this and seek to reverse a process that is already underway. Extraordinary means can be antibiotics or surgery, among others.

For a Hindu, the perspective may be that one lives as long as one naturally can, and then accepts the end as and when it happens. If a person has suffered severe brain damage and there is no hope of recovery, there is no basis for prolonging life by artificial means under Hindu principles.

Under Jewish law there may be different steps permitted or proscribed depending on whether the actions taken are passive or active, but in most instances preservation of life is paramount. But the preservation of life is not always absolute so that appropriate Rabbinic authority should be consulted.

For many faiths, the complexity of the issues involved will require input and guidance from a religious adviser with knowledge of these issues. Addressing this well in advance of a problem actually occurring, and building the appropriate mechanisms into your health care proxy and living will, can greatly minimize the emotional trauma for a family dealing with this at a later date.

## EXAMPLE

Many religious faiths take issue with terminating life support based on a lack of quality of life. The view taken by some is that life in any form is sacred and must be preserved. If you have COPD, the likelihood of dementia may be small. This may or may not make the quality of life issue relevant to you, your family, or your designated agents. But it should be addressed directly and explicitly in your documents. This issue is particularly important within the context of provision of nutrition and hydration. Should nutrition and hydration be provided to you if you have advanced dementia and are unaware of your surroundings? For those facing the challenges of COPD, it critical that if you have a religious affiliation that you address the issues of intubation, ventilation, and so forth, as these can be extremely charged emotional issues. If you are an adherent of a Western religious faith, bear in mind that the biblical definition of death according to many hinges on the cessation of cardio-pulmonary function. So how this is interpreted, and what steps might be optional or mandated, could be vital. According to some faiths, intentionally determining not to place someone on a ventilator could be tantamount to murder. Defining specific religious beliefs and practices is well beyond the scope of this book, but the vital point is that if you have any religious convictions or affiliations it is very important that you proactively address and deal with these concepts well in advance of them becoming real issues. You cannot expect your beliefs to be respected if you don't make them known. You owe it to your family and loved ones, however you choose to act with respect to these matters, to clarify your wishes to avoid them the heartache of arguing over what you would have wanted. And especially in light of COPD's impact and end-of-life decision making, this is more vital for you do address then perhaps for most other people.

## PREGNANCY AND MEDICAL DECISIONS

Every woman should carefully address the issues of pregnancy in her living will and/or health proxy because medical decision making concerning a mother and her fetus varies greatly among different religions. Generally Catholicism proscribes against taking direct action that would cause the death of an unborn child or the mother. You cannot choose the life of the mother over the life of the unborn child, or vice versa, since all life is sacred and that decision lies in God's hands alone. Unless this matter is expressly addressed in your living will, no one may know the degree of your devotion. You cannot expect health care providers to have the knowledge necessary to carry out your wishes without clear guidance from you. In contrast, under Jewish and Islamic law, saving the mother's life may generally given preference to saving the life of a fetus. If your illness may affect your pregnancy, you should discuss the possible additional risks and complications with your physician and, if appropriate, modify the provisions of your living will accordingly.

## PAIN RELIEF

Many patients and health care providers view the alleviation of all pain to be an essential and ideal objective. The nature of your chronic illness may have a profound impact on how you view this, but different religions view the concept of pain differently. For an Orthodox Christian, the act of suffering can mean purification, redemption, and salvation. While suffering is clearly not encouraged, pain relief that renders people unconscious during their last days may prevent them from partaking in profound and moving observances essential to their religious beliefs. The Christian Orthodox Church encourages you to be lucid during your last days so that you may confess sins and receive Holy Communion. If the attending physicians are not aware of this, they cannot be assumed to respect and foster this type of care. Similarly, according to Buddhist tradition, your consciousness near death directly correlates to the level of rebirth. Excessive pain relief could undermine this. However, Buddhists also believe that suffering is the converse of the optimal state of being. A sensitive balancing of important religious goals and your wishes in light of your current and future health status is thus required.

## FUNERAL AND OTHER POST-DEATH ARRANGEMENTS

Most religions provide for specific post-death rituals. Under Jewish law, autopsies and embalming are generally prohibited. In Buddhist tradition, it is a common belief that incense should be burned near a person close to death, to guide your last thoughts upward toward enlightenment. Some Buddhists believe that for a period following death, for a minimum of at least one week, the spirit may remain with the body and the body should therefore not be moved. Because these traditions may be impossible to carry out in almost any American medical or health care facility, people who wish to meet death according to these rites and rituals should consider making advance arrangements to spend their last days in a hospice sensitive to these religious beliefs, or at home. Some religions prohibit cremation, other religions or cultures favor it. These issues can be addressed in your living will, health proxy, and in some instances in your will (if, for example, you choose to be buried in another country or under other circumstances that create considerable cost).

## DISPOSITION OF ASSETS ON DEATH

A secular will may have to be modified to reflect the Baha'i, Jewish, Islamic, or other religious laws of inheritance. The Quran and Old Testament include detailed provisions as to how inheritance must be handled. While some of these provisions are similar, they are typically addressed quite differently in will drafting and should, in any case, be coordinated with tax, estate, financial and succession planning, and ethical issues. For the Christian Orthodox, not providing for family and relatives is tantamount to disowning your faith. For Catholics, there are general but vital guidelines regarding charity and justice.

## DISPUTE RESOLUTION

For all faiths, disputes of a religious or spiritual nature are perhaps best resolved through mandatory arbitration before a designated religious body, not a secular court. Both Buddhism and the Baha'i faith incorporate principles that affect how disputes should be addressed. The disinheritance of an heir and the use of in-terrorem clauses need to be evaluated. The Buddhist theory of Karma provides that everything done in a particular life, as well as in past lives, influences and affects future lives. If you disinherit an heir out of anger, it can be viewed as creating a negative influence that may be carried on through rebirth to the next life. Buddhism advocates that you take action out of compassion and not anger.

# WILL CHALLENGES AND OTHER LAWSUITS

Chronic illness is assumed by many to bring debilitation and incompetence. Regardless of the appropriateness of such assumptions to your situation, these generalizations and misconceptions make a challenge of your will (called a "will challenge") or of your other documents or planning, quite possible. The following two examples, each told from a different child's perspective, highlight the potential for challenges and lawsuits. See the discussion in Chapter 3.

### EXAMPLE 1: DAUGHTER'S PERSPECTIVE

Rebecca is 76 years old, lives in Connecticut, and has been diagnosed with severe COPD. Rebecca has two children, Joan (the older) and Tom (the younger). Joan lives nearby and has helped her mother for years with household chores and bill paying. Tom lives in Nevada and is quite busy with his young family and career. There has always been jealousy between Joan and Tom. As Rebecca's situation has worsened, Joan gave up a promotion and substantial raise with her company because she felt it imperative to stay in Connecticut to help her mother. The relocation to Florida that the promotion would have required would have made caregiving impossible. Rebecca realized the sacrifices that Joan was making. In time, she decided to retitle several large accounts as joint accounts in both their names. After a recent flare-up and related surgery, it has grown increasingly difficult for Rebecca to get around and to focus for extended periods of time on complex tasks. She had Joan change these accounts using the power of attorney that Rebecca's independent attorney prepared, naming Joan as agent. As Rebecca's COPD has progressed, while still quite aware, her mental acuity has declined to the point where she was no longer competent to make complex or involved decisions. Joan continued to care for her at the expense of her own career and social life. Since Rebecca had made it clear to Joan that she wanted her to inherit the joint accounts, Joan used other accounts to pay for Rebecca's expenses. By the time Rebecca died, the only assets left besides her home were the joint accounts with Joan. This was exactly what Rebecca wanted.

### EXAMPLE 2: SON'S PERSPECTIVE

As Rebecca's COPD progressed, her daughter Joan, who never really pursued a career with any vigor, forced herself on her mother and began to control her and her finances. While he cannot prove it Tom really believes that the stress Joan's interference and "pushy-ness" created for Rebecca helped trigger the recent flare-up that began a more pronounced decline. Rebecca realized the sacrifices that Tom had made to build his family and career and had always promised him help with his children's college costs. To prevent this from happening, after their mother already had lost some decision-making capacity but most significantly as she became more dependent on Joan, his sister Joan moved in for the kill. Joan, unbeknownst to her mother or brother, surreptitiously used a power of attorney to retitle several large accounts as joint accounts naming herself and her mother, so she would inherit them on her mother's death and so the accounts would avoid probate, which might give her brother Tom a better chance to challenge them. As Rebecca's COPD progressed, she really didn't have the strength or vigor to monitor these accounts, so Joan used Rebecca's remaining accounts to pay for part-time caregiving with the intent of depleting any resources that Tom could inherit. Although Rebecca had made it clear to Tom that she wanted him to inherit extra funds to pay for his children's college, Joan used other accounts to pay for Rebecca's expenses. By the time Rebecca died, other than her home, the only assets left were the joint accounts with Joan. This was exactly the opposite of what Rebecca wanted.

Planning to document gifts, restricting gifts under powers of attorney, mandating equal gifts, coordinating title to assets, actions of agents under powers and dispositive provisions under wills and trusts, takes on greater importance if you have a chronic illness, and especially if that illness brings any cognitive dysfunction. Annual (or even more frequent) meetings with your advisers to monitor these matters and document your intent while you are able can be vital to securing your wishes. Steps that you might consider include:

❖   *Revise and re-sign your will.* If you have no or only limited cognitive impact and you are clearly competent, have your attorney add a few modifications to your prior will and supervise your re-signing the will with different witnesses from those who witnessed you signing your last will. Making a change demonstrates that you revisited and reconsidered your will. Re-signing with new witnesses and a different notary creates a pattern to demonstrate your intent in the event of a will challenge. If the most recent will is held invalid as a result of a challenge, the will signed some months earlier with nearly identical primary dispositive provisions will be reinstated.

❖   *Beneficiaries should not be present.* Be certain that the caregiver and anyone else receiving a bequest are not present when documents are signed and corroborate this fact.

❖ *Document and explain unequal or unnatural bequests.* If the dispositive provision favors a particular heir, especially if that heir is the caregiver, explain and document in writing the reasoning for the disparate bequests. Have the caregiver/heir log his or her hours/efforts with an ongoing diary, and have an independent accountant estimate the economic cost (to the caregiver) of providing services.

❖ *Details.* List all family members' names and relationships in your will, and expressly name anyone to whom you are intentionally not making a bequest to avoid a challenge on the basis of the scrivener having left out that particular heir.

❖ *Prove competency.* Your attorney should take independent steps to corroborate your mental capacity at the time any document is signed.

## CHAPTER SUMMARY

Estate planning is not just about the obvious documents you need to sign. There are a number of ancillary issues that may be important to carrying out your wishes. Use your planners to identify the ones pertinent to you and what steps need to be taken on your behalf. If there are other issues important to you that are not mentioned, be vocal and tell your advisers about them.

## CHAPTER 13

# GETTING STARTED

## HOW TO USE THIS BOOK AS A WORKBOOK TO PLAN YOUR ESTATE AND DOCUMENTS

ESTATE AND FINANCIAL PLANNING FOR PEOPLE WITH COPD provides valuable tips and information on how to tailor your estate planning documents, and financial planning, to deal with the realities of COPD and for some of your personal or special considerations. Because many of the issues raised here concern complex matters, it is a good idea to discuss those that apply to your unique needs with your estate planning attorney. Address with your attorney all your wishes regarding your health care proxy, living will, HIPAA release, power of attorney, charitable planning, your will, and (if appropriate) a revocable living trust. Also talk with your attorney about the numerous ways your chronic disease may affect specific legal documents that should be prepared to safeguard you and those important to you. If hiring an attorney is not in your budget, you can use the sample forms in this book, forms found on www.chronicillnessplanning.org and www.laweasy.com, and forms that may be mandated by your state's statutes (laws). But never rely on any Internet forms without having a professional practicing in your state review them.

Make lists of the points from this book that apply to you and explain (to yourself and your attorney) how you think the recommendations or suggested language in the documents contained in the chapter appendices of this book should be tailored or changed to fit your personal circumstances. If you feel that the forms presented here do not adequately address your needs, write your questions or comments in the margins and ask your estate planner to help you address any necessary modifications. Remember that your final documents should reflect all relevant issues that are of concern to you, today and in the future if the progression of your chronic illness indicates that change is likely to occur.

Whatever your decisions, give serious thought to supplementing the legal documents with a heartfelt letter that sets forth and elaborates on your feelings about all the issues relevant to your circumstances. Although such a letter is not legally binding, it can go a long way to guiding your loved ones in carrying out your wishes, especially if the time comes when you are no longer able to communicate those wishes.

## HOW FORMS BECOME FINAL DOCUMENTS

Samples of the following forms have been included at the ends of chapters in this book to help you begin thinking about the decisions you must make and to help you "get the ball rolling":

❖   Power of Attorney

❖   HIPAA Release

❖   Living Will

❖   Health Care Proxy (or Medical Power of Attorney)

The book also includes sample provisions you can add to your revocable living trust. Getting the forms is just the first step. The next step is to discuss the forms and the sample provisions and any modifications you think might be necessary with your attorney. Note that many of the documents you need will probably not have to be created from scratch because your attorney undoubtedly will have his or her own standard forms. It will be less costly and less complicated for your attorney to make minor (in terms of drafting, not impact) modifications to his or her standard forms then draft an entirely new document. An added advantage to this is that your attorney's standard forms will already be tailored to accommodate your state's laws.

## WHY HIRING AN ATTORNEY IS THE BEST WAY TO GO

This section heading may sound like a self-serving plug from an attorney, but it really is sound advice. Think about it. You most likely don't prescribe your own medication—you leave this to a competent professional who is qualified to administer to your physical needs. By the same token, you should not prescribe your own complex legal decisions unless you are an attorney specializing in estate planning.

An attorney will take care of all document preparation for you and supervise your signing of those documents. This is by far the best approach, but remember that you are entitled and encouraged to express your opinions, concerns, and preferences about the issues that matter most to you. Also note that most lawyers have a comfort level with their own forms, templates, and language. That is fine as long as they tailor them to fully address your personal situation and the ramifications of your chronic illness.

If you cannot afford an attorney, follow the steps below to increase the likelihood that your documents will be effective. The word "likelihood" is used here deliberately. The tremendous variations in the laws of different states, the need for objective legal reasoning, the formalities of signing documents, and other complex matters are really difficult for you to address properly on your own, and a do-it-yourself approach can leave you vulnerable.

## IF YOU CANNOT AFFORD AN ATTORNEY

Because there is no substitute for getting qualified legal assistance to safeguard yourself, your assets, and your loved ones, if your financial situation does not allow you to hire an attorney, you should contact organizations that offer services to people with COPD: if you are old enough, contact senior citizen help organizations or your county Bar Association. Such organizations may be able to offer assistance.

## IF YOU CANNOT GET ANY PROFESSIONAL HELP

If your efforts to get professional assistance do not succeed, your last resort may be to tackle the matter yourself. Use the ideas in this book. Watch the videos and PowerPoint presentations on www.chronicillnessplanning.org. Then obtain sample documents and forms and sample provisions from this book and the following free websites: www.chronicillnessplanning.org and www.laweasy.com. Hopefully you have made notes to yourself while reading this book that you can use to help you mark more comprehensive notes on these forms. Then, after that homework and preparation, use an online legal document preparation service. Be sure to type in all relevant information, changes, and corrections that are pertinent to you. If you don't have access to a computer, or have trouble typing, ask a friend to help you. When you have completed the forms, print and carefully review them. (It is easier to spot mistakes on a hard copy than on a computer screen.) The final draft of your documents should not have corrections penned in. Make all revisions on the computer and print clean final documents reflecting all the changes you've made. Once that has been done, staple the form twice, once on the top left corner, and once on the top right corner. *NEVER* remove the staples from the document you print. It may invalidate it.

## HOW TO SIGN FINAL DOCUMENTS

Be aware that state laws differ significantly on this point and should be reviewed before any documents are signed and/or filed. As discussed in an earlier chapter, you can find this information in the reference section of your local library. Use the index to find the specific information you need, but ask the librarian to show you the updates, often called "pocket parts," that typically appear at the end of each volume. You can also try to find this information online. Hopefully, any online document preparation website you use will have properly researched these issues. The best bet is to verify what is required. If it seems uncertain, opt for the highest standard you see indicated. For example, if you see a reference to a notary and two witnesses that isn't clear, be sure the notary is not a witness so that you have in effect three, not two, people involved. If the statements of what the law is are not clear to you, interpret them in the manner that is the most strict possible.

Once your documents are prepared, there are several steps you must take to ensure that they are signed correctly and legally. Arrange to have two or three (depending on the forms) witnesses and a notary. None of the witnesses or the notary should be people named in the documents; also, they should not be related to you. Once you are all assembled in a clean quiet area, lay out each document. Then review and discuss the documents. Finally, sign them in front of each other (you should sign in the presence of the witnesses and notary and the witnesses should sign in front of you and each other). No one may leave the room during the signing process. Be sure to identify each document prior to signing it. Explain what the document accomplishes and why you are signing it. Before signing your will and revocable living trust (if you are using one), identify to the witnesses and notary all of the people you have named in these documents, describe your key assets, and explain in general terms how each document distributes these assets to the people you've named.

When you, the witnesses, and notary are signing the documents, be sure to carefully read the notations under the signature lines and carefully follow the prompts listed in each form.

# ONCE YOU'RE DONE, WHAT'S NEXT?

Once you have signed your documents, you must decide where they go:

❖     All original documents should be stored in a secure, fireproof location that is accessible to those who will serve as your agents and other fiduciaries.

❖     Prepare photocopies of the documents for each of your key advisers and fiduciaries. Don't unstaple the documents. Copy them by flipping each page one at a time so that the staples aren't disturbed.

❖     Sign only one copy of your will, and keep that original, preferably in a fireproof safe in your house.

❖     Some attorneys might suggest you sign multiple originals of your living trust, but given the length of the document it's probably more practical to sign one original and distribute copies. Other attorneys might caution you to sign only one. However, if you've named a bank as trustee, the bank may want an original (but if you have enough assets that a bank or trust company will serve as trustee, you can also afford an attorney to do this).

❖     You may sign several original copies of your power of attorney, and if you truly trust your agent, you can give him or her a signed original. One copy should always be kept in a fireproof safe in your house, and one should be kept elsewhere (e.g., a safe deposit box).

❖     Sign several originals of the HIPAA release, health care proxy, and living will. You should always give at least one original of each to your health care agent. If your first agent is someone living with you, it is a good idea to give a second original to someone named as a successor agent and who lives elsewhere. You should also give your doctor or health care provider a photocopy to include with your medical records. One copy should always be kept at home in an easily and quickly accessible location in case of emergency.

❖     Scan copies of all of these documents and have them backed up using an online service and ideally back up your entire laptop and store that backup in a secure location outside your home.

## ANNUAL REVIEW AND FOLLOW-UP

While some illnesses take a severe toll quite quickly, most chronic illnesses progress over time, affording you opportunities to revisit and refine your planning. Use these opportunities wisely. Annual reviews can ensure that new issues can be addressed, old decisions can be re-evaluated, and changes in circumstances and new legal developments can be incorporated. It is likely that your views and feelings about a range of issues (from personal care, to agents you have named, to other aspects of planning) will evolve as your illness lingers or progresses.

## CHAPTER SUMMARY

This chapter addressed the final step in the estate planning process. Once you've thought through all your issues and made all your decisions, the final step is to complete and sign your documents. Great care should be taken in doing so. If there is any way in which you can obtain help from an attorney, ideally one specializing in estate planning, that will be the best for you. Whatever approach you use, great attention to detail and formalities are essential.

# INDEX